Grammar Tools Made Easy

(The easiest way to learn English and French)

All the logical information we know instinctively about English and French combined

Grammar Tools Made Easy

(The easiest way to learn English and French)

Grammar Tools Made Easy was written from the inspiration I received from all my students who compelled me to become the best English teacher I could be.

Thanks to all of my students in Québec City, Canada. Without you this book would not have been possible.

AuthorHouse™
1663 Liberty Drive
Bloomington, IN 47403
www.authorhouse.com
Phone: 1-800-839-8640

Published by AuthorHouse 2/2/2012

ISBN: 978-1-4670-6305-0 (sc)
ISBN: 978-1-4670-6303-6 (e)

Library of Congress Control Number: 2011960094

INTRODUCTION

Grammar Tools Made Easy (*The easiest way to learn English and French*) is a reference guide to understanding the connections between English and French. It is a practical guide to ensure that you understand your mother tongue as well as learning a second language at the same time. It can be used to fully comprehend the similarities between English and French with references to the tenses as well as the basic grammar points between the two languages.

Level

This book takes you from the beginning of the two languages fully covering basic grammar points to much more advanced grammar points. It demonstrates the similarities and the differences between English and French. Knowing that both languages come from "romance languages" better known as Latin, they are fully interconnected and easier to learn if and once you are aware of your mother tongue. Having all the information we need instinctively, we can use these tools along with this book to guide you to fully understand the connection between the two languages. This book outlines the general mistakes made between the two languages. It is a helpful guide to the easiest way to speak and understand English or French. This book is designed to help beginner students as well as advanced students who may want to refine their language skills.

How this book is Organized

This book is composed of 80 units that completely outline each grammar point. Starting from the front to the back cover this book clearly explains the grammar points necessary to understand and speak English or French. As you work your way through this book each unit gets more and more challenging, making it imperative to understand the previous unit before moving to the next. The Contents at the beginning of the book provides a list of units detailing each unit's contents. There are also 5 Appendices at the end of the book with a list of "Irregular Verbs" in English for a quick reference followed by a complete *Index* and *Glossary*.

Using this book

It is *not* necessary to follow this book step by step if you already have a base in English or French. It is for the teacher to decide along with the students what grammar points to focus on and how much time is needed to master each grammar point. This book can be used on an individual basis or in a classroom setting. Although this book is intended to make English or French more easily understood, you will need to follow courses. Native English speakers will have to have a «Bescherelle» for the conjugation of French verbs and a dictionary handy to improve your vocabulary. Native French speakers will have to have a good dictionary not only for vocabulary but also for *phrasal verbs*. If any student has difficulty understanding the contents of this book check with your teacher for further explanation.

INTRODUCTION

Grammar Tools Made Easy (*La façon la plus facile d'apprendre l'anglais et le français*) est un guide de référence permettant d'apprendre l'anglais et le français par la comparaison entre les deux langues. Il s'agit d'un guide pratique qui permet une compréhension logique de la langue maternelle aussi bien que de la langue seconde. À partir des similarités entre les deux langues, ce livre aide à comprendre les points communs entre les grammaires anglaise et française.

Niveau

Ce livre commence avec le niveau débutant et offre une progression jusqu'à un niveau avancé. Il favorise l'apprentissage en mettant en évidence les similitudes et les différences entre l'anglais et le français. À partir du moment où l'on prend conscience des règles de base de notre langue maternelle et sachant que ces deux langues proviennent toutes deux de la même racine latine, on comprend qu'elles sont étroitement liées et, par le fait même, plus facile à apprendre. Nous avons tous une connaissance instinctive de notre langue maternelle et les outils de comparaison que nous propose cette grammaire permettront à la fois de mieux maîtriser la première langue et celle en apprentissage. En soulignant les erreurs de traduction fréquentes entre l'anglais et le français, ce guide propose une méthode facile pour parler et comprendre ces deux langues. Il s'adresse autant au débutant qu'à l'étudiant plus avancé désirant raffiner son niveau de langage.

Structure du livre

Ce livre est composé de 80 étapes traitant des règles de grammaire. Du début à la fin, il fournit tous les outils nécessaires pour comprendre et parler l'anglais ou le français. Au fur et à mesure que l'on avance dans la lecture, les règles se complexifient. Il est donc nécessaire de comprendre pleinement une étape avant de passer à la suivante. *La table* des matières apparaissant au début du livre énumère et détaille le contenu de chaque étape. Cinq annexes apparaissent également à la toute fin, comprenant la liste des verbes irréguliers pour une référence rapide ainsi qu'un *index* complet et un *glossaire*.

Comment utiliser ce livre

Il n'est pas nécessaire de suivre ce livre de façon linéaire si vous avez déjà un certain niveau de connaissance en anglais ou en français. Il appartient au professeur de décider avec les étudiants quelles sont les règles de grammaire à approfondir et le temps nécessaire pour réaliser chaque étape. Ce livre peut être utilisé sur une base individuelle ou bien en groupe. Même s'il a été rédigé afin de rendre la compréhension de l'anglais et du français plus facile, il est recommandé de suivre un cours de langue en complémentarité. Les anglophones devront avoir un «Bescherelle» pour la conjugaison des verbes français ainsi qu'un dictionnaire de poche afin d'améliorer leur vocabulaire. Les francophones devront avoir un bon dictionnaire, non seulement pour acquérir un vocabulaire juste et varié, mais également pour apprendre les *phrasal verbs*.

CONTENTS

CONTENTS

CONTENTS

To be/être	Verb and Auxiliary	Present - Past - Future
I am I was I will be	1st person singular	Je suis J'étais Je serai
You are You were You will be	2nd person singular	Tu es Tu étais Tu seras
He is He was He will be	3rd person singular	Il est Il était Il sera
She is She was She will be	3rd person singular	Elle est Elle était Elle sera
It is It was It will be	3rd person singular	Il est Il était Il sera
We are We were We will be	1st person plural	Nous sommes Nous étions Nous serons
You are You were You will be	2nd person plural	Vous êtes Vous étiez Vous serez
They are They were They will be	3rd person plural	Ils sont Ils étaient Ils seront
They are They were They will be	3rd person plural	Elles sont Elles étaient Elles seront

 Note: In English and in French the verbs *to be/être* are both a verb and an auxiliary.

Personal Notes

3

To have/avoir	Verb and Auxiliary	Present - Past - Future
I have I had I will have	1st person singular	J'ai J'avais J'aurai
You have You had You will have	2nd person singular	Tu as Tu avais Tu auras
He has He had He will have	3rd person singular	Il a Il avait Il aura
She has She had She will have	3rd person singular	Elle a Elle avait Elle aura
It has It had It will have	3rd person singular	Il a Il avait Il aura
We have We had We will have	1st person plural	Nous avons Nous avions Nous aurons
You have You had You will have	2nd person plural	Vous avez Vous aviez Vous aurez
They have They had They will have	3rd person plural	Ils ont Ils avaient Ils auront
They have They had They will have	3rd person plural	Elles ont Elles avaient Elles auront

 Note: In English and in French the verbs *to have/avoir* are both a verb and an auxiliary.

I do I did I will do	1st person singular	Je fais Je faisais Je ferai
You do You did You will do	2nd person singular	Tu fais Tu faisais Tu feras
He does He did He will do	3rd person singular	Il fait Il faisait Il fera
She does She did She will do	3rd person singular	Elle fait Elle faisait Elle fera
It does It did It will do	3rd person singular	Il fait Il faisait Il fera
We do We did We will do	1st person plural	Nous faisons Nous faisions Nous ferons
You do You did You will do	2nd person plural	Vous faites Vous faisiez Vous ferez
They do They did They will do	3rd person plural	Ils font Ils faisaient Ils feront
They do They did They will do	3rd person plural	Elles font Elles faisaient Elles feront

 Note: In English the verb *to do/faire* is both a verb and an auxiliary.

Positive	S	V	O	
	subject	verb	object	

Positive	S	V	L	
	subject	verb	location	

Positive	S	V	A	
	subject	verb	adjective	

Positive	S	A	V	O
	subject	auxiliary	verb	object

Negative	S	A	N	V	O
	subject	auxiliary	negative	verb	object

Questions	A	S	V	O
	auxiliary	subject	verb	object

Exceptions: In English the verb *to be* is the exception with *questions* and *negative sentence* structures. This *sentence structure VSO* for *questions* is used the same way in French. For *negative sentences* in English this *sentence structure* is used *SVNO* and in French the *sentence structure SNVNO* is used.

Exceptions: This *sentence structure* for *questions VSO* and the *sentence structure* for *negative sentences SVNO* is used in English for the *Simple Past* and *Simple Present only* when you use the verb *to be* as the verb.

Examples:

V	S	O		S	V	N	O
verb	subject	object		subject	verb	negative	object
Are	you	at work?		I	am	not	at work.
Êtes -	vous	au travail?		Je ne	suis	pas	au travail.
Were	you	there when I called?		I	was	not	there when you called.
Étais -	tu	là quand j'ai appelé?		Je n'	étais	pas	là quand tu as appelé.

Sentence Structures in French

Positive	S sujet	V verbe	C complément			

Positive	S sujet	V verbe	L lieu

Positive	S sujet	V verbe	A adjectif

Positive	S sujet	A auxiliaire	V verbe	C complément

Négative	S sujet	N négation	V verbe	N négation	C complément

Négative	S sujet	N négation	A auxiliaire	N négation	V verbe	C complément

Questions	A auxiliaire	S sujet	V verbe	C complément

Questions	V verbe	S sujet	C complément

 The *sentence structure VSO* for *questions* is the same in English and French for the *Simple Past* and *Simple Present only* when using the verb *to be* as the verb.

10

Infinitive Verbs/Les verbes infinitif

The *infinitive form* of a verb is the *raw form* of a verb *without* any conjugation. Conjugating a verb changes the tense of verb you are using. For example: past, present or future.

In English the *infinitive verb* is "*to* " followed by the verb.

 Examples: To eat   To do   To finish   To see

 Note: The *infinitive verbs* in French have different endings of each verb instead of "*to.* " You will need to consult a «*Bescherelle»* a book containing the conjugation for all French verbs to see the different endings of each verb used in each verb tense.

 Note: There are four columns of verb endings in French. Each verb column determines the conjugation of the verb. If the column is "*er* " then all the verbs in French ending with "*er* " will conjugate the same way having the same ending of each verb used in each tense. The columns are listed below.

 Examples: "er"   "re"   "ir"   "oir"

          manger   faire   finir   voir

 Note: These verbs in each column equal the *infinitive form* in English.

12

Personal

Notes

There are *exceptions* between English and French when you use the verb *to be* and the verb *to have* as the verb.

The verb *to be/être* is used to state a *fact* whereas the verb *to have/avoir* is used to talk about a *possession.*

To be	Exceptions:	To have
I am 30 years old		J'ai 30 ans
I am hungry		J'ai faim
I am thirsty		J'ai soif
I am cold		J'ai froid
I am hot		J'ai chaud
I am right		J'ai raison
I am looking forward to		J'ai hâte de
There is/there are		Il y a
There was/there were		Il y avait
There will be		Il y aura

 When using *to be/être* or *to have/avoir* with these adjectives be careful *not* to translate word by word. Use the verbs in the way shown above.

 The examples above are in 1st person singular and can also be used with all other subjects, you, he, she, we, you and they.

A *preposition* is a word used before a noun to *connect* it to other words.

in	at	on	to
dans	à	sur	à/vers

 Note: In French to use a *preposition* you first need to determine if the noun is masculin, féminin or pluriel, then correspond the *preposition* to the noun. In English when using *at, in* and *to* make sure you correspond the *preposition* to the verb. Use *at* or *in* with verbs of *no* movement and use *to* with verbs of movement.

à/au/aux   = at   =   building or event with verbs of *no* movement

à/au/aux/en = in   =   a city, town or country with verbs of *no* movement

à/au/aux/en = to   =   verbs of movement

 Note: Verbs of *no* movement mean you stay in one place. For example: stay, live, work, have and study etc.

 Examples: I saw you at the movies last night.
Je t'ai vu au cinéma hier soir.

I live in Canada.
Je demeure au Canada.

Note: Verbs of movement mean you start at Point A and finish at Point B. For example: go, fly, drive, walk, run, give and say etc.

Examples: I go to work every day.
Je vais au travail chaque jour.

I walk to the library every week.
Je marche à la bibliothèque chaque semaine.

_____

_____

_____

_____

_____

_____

_____

_____

_____

_____

_____

_____

_____

_____

_____

_____

_____

_____

_____

_____

_____

_____

Again a *preposition* is a word used before a noun to connect it to other words.

 Examples:

in	at	on
dans	à	sur

 Note: In French to use a *preposition* you first need to determine if the noun is masculin, féminin or pluriel, then correspond the *preposition* to the noun. In English correspond the preposition *at* with being a specific time, *on* being a specific day or date and *in* being a period of time.

à	=	at	=	specific time
le	=	on	=	specific day or date
en	=	in	=	period of time

Examples:

Examples of a specific time	=	at 5:00pm/à 17h00 at 7:30am/à 07h30 at noon/à midi
Examples of a specific date	=	on May 10th/le 10 mai on June 25th/le 25 juin on August 5th/le 5 août
Examples of a period of time	=	in April/en avril in summer/en été in 2005/en 2005

Exceptions: Here are some of the *exceptions* between English and French using *prepositions* in other situations other than with *time.*

in the spring	au printemps
in a picture	sur une photo
on the ceiling	au plafond
on the first floor	au premier étage
on your left/right	à votre gauche/droite
at the top/at the bottom	en haut/en bas

In English and French *articles* are:

a	an	the
un/une	un/une	le/la/les

Again, when using an *article* in French you first need to determine if the object is masculin, féminin or pluriel, then correspond the *article* to the object. In English correspond *a* with a *general* object, *an* with a *general* object that starts with a vowel and *the* with a *singular* or *plural specific* object.

 A or *an* = a *singular general* object in English however in French it depends on if the object is masculin (un) or féminin (une).

 A = a *singular general* object

a book
un livre

An = a *singular general* object used before a *vowel*

an apple
une pomme

 The = either a *singular* or *plural specific* object in English however in French it depends on if the object is masculin (le), féminin (la) or pluriel (les).

 The = a *singular* or *plural specific* object

the book
le livre

the apples
les pommes

 Every *object* is either masculin, féminin or pluriel in French so the *article* changes depending on the *object.*

 When an *object* is plural in English it is important to pronounce the "*s* " unlike in French where most of the time the "*s* " is *not* pronounced.

Adjectives

In English when using the adjectives *this, that, these* and *those* it depends if the object is *singular* or *plural* and how *close* or *far* the object or objects are to you. In French it does *not* matter whether or *not* the object is *close* or *far* from you it only matters if the object is masculin, féminin or pluriel.

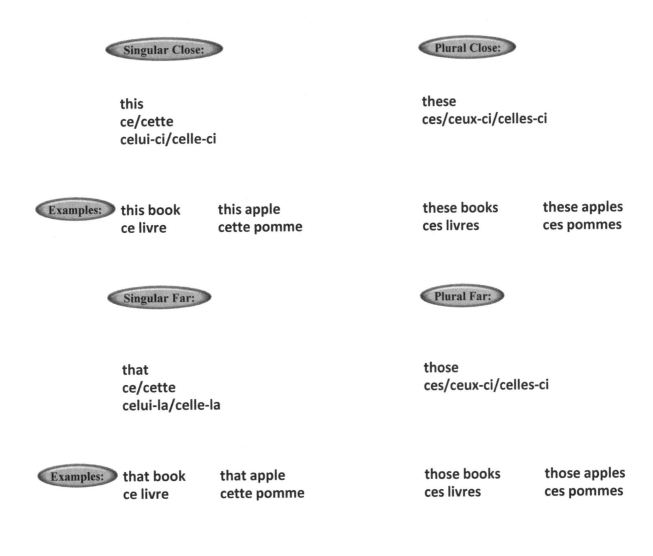

Singular Close:

this
ce/cette
celui-ci/celle-ci

Plural Close:

these
ces/ceux-ci/celles-ci

Examples: | this book | this apple
ce livre | cette pomme

these books | these apples
ces livres | ces pommes

Singular Far:

that
ce/cette
celui-la/celle-la

Plural Far:

those
ces/ceux-ci/celles-ci

Examples: | that book | that apple
ce livre | cette pomme

those books | those apples
ces livres | ces pommes

Note: "*Ce/celui-ci*" are masculin and "*cette/celle-ci*" are féminin.

Note: "*Ces/ceux-ci*" are masculin pluriel and "*ces/celles-ci*" are féminin pluriel.

as a	en tant que	since/because	puisque
as....as	aussi.....que	so	tellement
as for	quant à	therefore	donc
as if	comme si	then	alors
although	bien que	though	bien que
anybody	personne	whatever	quoique/ n'importe quoi
anyhow	n'importe comment qu'importe	whenever	n'importe quand
anymore	ne.....plus	whereabouts	où (donc)
anyway	de toute façon	whereas	alors que
anywhere	n'importe où	whether	si
by the way	au fait	whichever	quel/quelle que soit...(que)
However	comment (donc)/ cependant	while	pendant que
Of course	bien sûr	whoever	quiconque/qui (donc)

Personal Notes

All of these adverbs or pronouns can be used in front of a *question* to find out the *information* being asked. These are known as *information questions.*

who	qui
where	où
when	quand
why	pourquoi
what	quoi
how	comment
which	quel/quelle

 Note: Use the sentence structure *Information ASVO* in English.

 Examples:

Where do you live?

How do you do that?

Why are you doing that?

 Note: There are several ways to ask an *information question* in French.

Information VS   *Information ASVO*   *Information SVCO*

 Examples:

Où demeurez-vous?

Comment est-ce que tu fais cela?

Pourquoi tu fais cela?

 Note: The sentence structure *Information SVCO* in French is used for spoken French whereas in written French to state the same *information question* the sentence structure is *VSC.*

Possessive adjectives are used to modify a noun to state that an *object* or a *person* belongs to someone or something.

 Examples:

my	mon/ma/mes	my mom	ma mère
your	ton/ta/tes	your dad	ton père
his	son/sa/ses	his sister	sa soeur
her	son/sa/ses	her brother	son frère
our	notre/nos	our house	notre maison
your	votre/vos	your keys	vos clés
their	leur/leurs	their books	leurs livres

 Note: When using a *possessive adjective* in French you need to correspond the *possessive adjective* to the *object* in the sentence and *not* to the *subject* as in English.

 Examples:

He washes his car every week.	He broke his computer last year.
Il lave sa voiture chaque semaine.	Il a brisé son ordinateur l'année passée.
She washes her car every week.	She broke her computer last year.
Elle lave sa voiture chaque semaine.	Elle a brisé son ordinateur l'année passée.

 Note: Because there are *no* masculin or féminin objects in English it is impossible to correspond the *possessive adjective* to the *object* thus the *possessive adjective* corresponds to the *subject*.

In English there are 6 *Basic tenses* and 6 *Perfect tenses*. In French there are 4 *Simple tenses* that equal the English *Basic tenses* and 4 *Compound tenses* which equal the *Perfect tenses* in English.

 Note: The English tenses are listed first followed by the French equivalent tense.

Basic tenses/Simple tenses	Perfect tenses/Compound tenses
Simple Past/passé simple	Past Perfect/plus-que-parfait
Past Continuous/imparfait	Past Perfect Continuous/imparfait + depuis
Simple Present/présent de l'indicatif	Present Perfect/passé composé
Present Continuous/présent de l'indicatif	Present Perfect Continuous/présent + depuis
Simple Future/futur simple	Future Perfect/futur antérieur
Future Continuous/sera + en train de	Future Perfect Continuous/ça fera + présent

 Note: In English and in French there are other *tenses* as well listed at the bottom of this page. The verb tenses listed above represent *time* whereras the verb *tenses* listed below represent a *mood, suggestion* or *order*.

Conditional/conditionnel	Subjunctive/présent du subjonctif
Past Conditional/conditionnel passé	imparfait du subjonctif
Imperative/impératif	passé du subjonctif
	plus-que-parfait du subjonctif

Simple Past or *passé simple* in French is used to talk about an action in the past that is over.

1. An action in the past that is finished.	1. Une action dans le passé qui est finie.
2. We know when the action happened.	2. Nous savons quand l'action est arrivée.
3. The time is finished.	3. Le temps est fini.
4. There is *no* connection to the present.	4. Il n'y a aucun raccordement au présent.
5. The action did *not* happen in a *duration* of time *until now.*	5. L'action n'est pas arrivée dans une *durée* de temps *jusqu'à maintenant.*

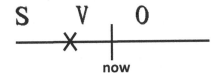

Key Words: Key words that make the action in the *past* are listed below.

yesterday	last	ago	when	this
hier	dernier	il y a	quand	ce/cette

Examples:

I went to Québec last year.
J'allai à Québec l'année passée.

I did my homework yesterday.
Je fis mes devoirs hier.

 Note: When speaking or writing English "*I have done «j'ai fait» my homework yesterday* " does *not* exist like in French, you have to say "*I did «je fis» my homework yesterday.* "

I went to Québec last year.
Je suis allé à Québec l'année passée.

I did my homework yesterday.
J'ai fait mes devoirs hier.

 Note: When speaking French you need to use the tense *passé composé* instead of using *passé simple* as *passé simple* is used more commonly for formal written French.

 Note: For a comparison between *Simple Past/passé simple* and *Present Perfect/ passé composé* see unit 34.

Past Continuous or *imparfait* in French is used to talk about an action that was in *progress* when a second action happened *at the same time* to *interrupt* the first action.

 The formula to conjugate *Continuous tenses* (*to be* + *verb* + *ing*) is used in English and in French. In addition to conjugating this tense in French using le *verbe être* au *passé* + *en train de* + *l'infinitif (SAVC)* you can also use *imparfait (SVC)* which gives the same meaning.

S   A   V   O

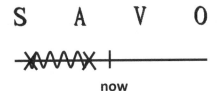

now

I was	+	VERB	+	ing		J'étais	+	en train de	+	VERBE
You were	+	VERB	+	ing		Tu étais	+	en train de	+	VERBE
He was	+	VERB	+	ing		Il était	+	en train de	+	VERBE
We were	+	VERB	+	ing		Nous étions	+	en train de	+	VERBE
You were	+	VERB	+	ing		Vous étiez	+	en train de	+	VERBE
They were	+	VERB	+	ing		Ils étaient	+	en train de	+	VERBE

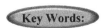 Key words that make the action in the *past* are listed below.

| yesterday | last | ago | when |
| hier | dernier | il y a | quand |

 When in English and *lorsque/quand* in French connects the first action to the second action.

 I was doing my homework when the phone rang.
J'étais en train de faire mes devoirs lorsque le téléphone a sonné.

I was doing my homework when the phone rang.
Je faisais mes devoirs lorsque le téléphone a sonné.

Unit 18   Simple Present

The *Simple Present* or *présent de l'indicatif* in French is used to talk about a *routine*. A *routine* is something that is done *regularly* or in *specified intervals*.

Note: If an action is a *daily routine* then the action happened yesterday, two days ago etc. So if the *routine* continues the action will happen tomorrow. The action is *not* in *progress* at the time of speaking.

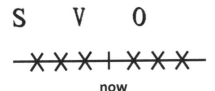

now

Key Words: Key words that make the action a *routine* are listed below.

every day	each month	often	usually
chaque jour	chaque mois	souvent	habituellement
Mondays	sometimes	always	the weekends
les lundis	parfois	toujours	les fins de semaine

Examples:

I go to work every day.
Je vais au travail chaque jour.

You drink a coffee every morning.
Tu bois un café chaque matin.

He eats an apple every day.
Il mange une pomme chaque jour.

We do our homework every night.
Nous faisons nos devoirs chaque soir.

You drive a 1000 kilometers a month.
Vous conduisez mille kilomètres par mois.

They take the bus often.
Ils prennent l'autobus souvent.

Note: In English for the *Simple Present tense only* the verb conjugation for *3rd person singular* is adding an "*s*" to the verb. In French each verb ending changes depending on the *subject*. In English, if you do *not* pronounce the "*s*" for *3rd person singular* "*he eat*" then the sound will be like "*nous mange/vous mange*" in French. See examples below.

Examples:

I eat	Je mange	I go	Je vais
You eat	Tu manges	You go	Tu vas
He eats	Il mange	He goes	Il va
We eat	Nous mangeons	We go	Nous allons
You eat	Vous mangez	You go	Vous allez
They eat	Ils mangent	They go	Ils vont

The *Present Continuous* or *présent de l'indicatif* in French is used to talk about an action that is in *progress* which is happening at the time of speaking.

 Note: The formula to conjugate *Continuous tenses* (*to be* + *verb* + *ing*) is used in English and in French. In addition to conjugating this tense in French using le *verbe être* au *présent* + *en train de* + *l'infinitif (SAVC)* you can also use the *présent de l'indicatif (SVC)* which gives the same meaning.

S   A   V   O

————————✳————————

now

I am	+	VERB	+	ing
You are	+	VERB	+	ing
He is	+	VERB	+	ing
We are	+	VERB	+	ing
You are	+	VERB	+	ing
They are	+	VERB	+	ing

Je suis	+	en train de	+	VERBE
Tu es	+	en train de	+	VERBE
Il est	+	en train de	+	VERBE
Nous sommes	+	en train de	+	VERBE
Vous êtes	+	en train de	+	VERBE
Ils sont	+	en train de	+	VERBE

Key Words: Key words that make the action in *progress now* are listed below.

| now | presently | at this moment |
| maintenant | présentement | à ce moment |

verbe au présent

être au présent + *en train de* + *l'infinitif*

Examples:

I am working now.
Je travaille maintenant.

I am working now.
Je suis en train de travailler maintenant.

I am doing my homework.
Je fais mes devoirs.

I am doing my homework.
Je suis en train de faire mes devoirs.

Note: The *Present Continuous tense* can also have a double meaning. It can be used to state a *previous engagement* meaning you have already made a reservation to do the action at a later date.

Examples:

Are you playing golf tomorrow?
Joues-tu au golf demain?

I am going to Mexico this year.
Je vais au Mexique cette année.

The *Simple Future* or *futur simple* in French is used to talk about an action that *will* happen in the future.

The verb conjugation in French is the ending of the verb using 1st person "*rai* " 2nd person "*ras* " 3rd person "*ra* " 1st person plural "*rons* " 2nd person plural "*rez* " 3rd person plural "*ront.* " These endings of the verb are equal to the auxiliary "*will* " in English.

 Note: In English *will* is used as the auxiliary in front of the *base form* of the verb equaling the sentence structure *SAVO.* In French the sentence structure for *futur simple* is *SVC.*

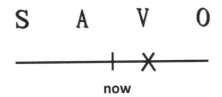

S   A   V   O

now

 **Key Words:** Key words that make the action in the *future* are listed below.

tomorrow	later	in	after	next
demain	plus tard	dans	après	le prochain
				la prochaine

 Note: *Simple Future* is an action that *will* 100% happen in the future and is considered to be an *intention.* The action in the *Simple Future tense* is decided at the time of speaking and is *not foreseen* or *planned.*

 Examples:

I will go to work tomorrow.	J'irai au travail demain.
You will go to work tomorrow.	Tu iras au travail demain.
He will go to work tomorrow.	Il ira au travail demain.
We will go to work tomorrow.	Nous irons au travail demain.
You will go to work tomorrow.	Vous irez au travail demain.
They will go to work tomorrow.	Ils iront au travail demain.

The *Future Continuous* or *sera en train de* in French is used to talk about an action in the future that will be in *progress* at a specific time.

In French there is *no* tense so we need to use the same formula as in English for the *Continuous tenses*, *(to be + verb + ing)* le *verbe être* au *futur + en train de + l'infinitif (SAVC).*

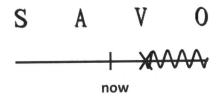

S   A   V   O

now

I will be	+	VERB	+	ing		Je serai	+	en train de	+	VERBE
You will be	+	VERB	+	ing		Tu seras	+	en train de	+	VERBE
He will be	+	VERB	+	ing		Il sera	+	en train de	+	VERBE
We will be	+	VERB	+	ing		Nous serons	+	en train de	+	VERBE
You will be	+	VERB	+	ing		Vous serez	+	en train de	+	VERBE
They will be	+	VERB	+	ing		Ils seront	+	en train de	+	VERBE

Key Words: Key words that make the action in the *future* are listed below.

at	later	tomorrow	next
à	plus tard	demain	le prochain
			la prochaine

| in | after | afterwards | |
| dans | après | plus tard | |

Examples:

At one o'clock, I will be teaching a class.
À 13h00, je serai en train d'enseigner un cours.

Nous serons en train de faire la vaisselle après le souper.
We will be doing the dishes after supper.

We know when we are speaking if the action that we are *going to* do is *foreseen* or *not.* If we have already made the decision to do the action this shows the difference between a *planned action* or something that is *not planned.*

In English use the *Present tense* of the verb *to be* followed by "*going to* " plus the *base form* of a verb. In French however use the verb *aller* au *présent* followed by *l'infinitif.*

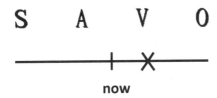

now

 When the action is *planned* before speaking the *Present Continuous with a Future Meaning* is used in English and *futur proche* is used in French. See examples below.

I am going to eat	Je vais manger
You are going to do	Tu vas faire
He is going to work	Il va travailler
We are going to watch	Nous allons regarder
You are going to take	Vous allez prendre
They are going to go	Ils vont aller

 When the action is *decided* at the time of speaking and is *not foreseen/prévu* the *Simple Future/futur simple* is used both in English and in French. See examples below.

I will eat	Je mangerai
You will do	Tu feras
He will work	Il travaillera
We will watch	Nous regarderons
You will take	Vous prendrez
They will go	Ils iront

In English if there is *no* auxiliary in the *affirmative sentence* use the verb *to do* as the *auxiliary.* The only exception is when you use the verb *to be* as the verb in the *Simple Present* and *Simple Past tenses.* See unit 4.

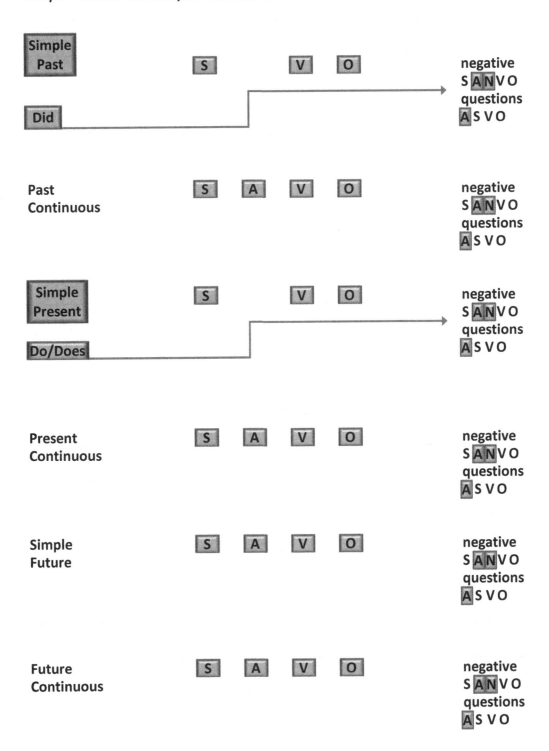

S   V O

Simple Past

I went to Montreal last weekend.
I did not go to Montreal last weekend.
Did you go to Montreal last weekend?

S A V O

Past Continuous

I was going to Montreal when I saw a bear.
I was not going to Montreal when I saw a bear.
Were you going to Montreal when you saw a bear?

S   V O

Simple Present

I go to Montreal every month.
I do not go to Montreal every month.
Do you go to Montreal every month?

S A V O

Present Continuous

I am going to Montreal right now.
I am not going to Montreal right now.
Are you going to Montreal right now?

S A V O

Simple Future

I will go to Montreal next month.
I will not go to Montreal next month.
Will you go to Montreal next month?

S A V O

Future Continuous

I will be going to Montreal at 5:00pm.
I will not be going to Montreal at 5:00pm.
Will you be going to Montreal at 5:00pm?

Sentence Structures in French for the Simple Tenses

passé simple

S | | | V | O
S | | A | V | O

négative
S N V N O
S N A N V O
question
A S V O

imparfait

S | | | V | O
S | | A | V | O

négative
S N V N O
S N A N V O
question
A S V O
V S O

présent de l'indicatif

S | | V | O

négative
S N V N O
question
A S V O
V S O

présent de l'indicatif

S | | | V | O
S | | A | V | O

négative
S N V N O
S N A N V O
question
A S V O
V S O

futur simple

S | | V | O

négative
S N V N O
question
A S V O
V S O

futur en progrès

S | A | V | O

négative
S N A N V O
question
A S V O

S V O

**passé
simple**

J'allai (je suis allé) à Montréal hier.
Je n'allai pas (je ne suis pas allé) à Montréal hier.
Est-ce que tu allas (tu es allé) à Montréal hier?

S V O

imparfait

J'allais (j'étais en train d'aller) à Montréal quand j'ai vu un ours.
Je n'allais pas à Montréal lorsque j'ai vu un ours.
Est-ce que tu allais à Montréal lorsque tu as vu un ours?

S V O

**présent
de l'indicatif**

Je vais à Montréal chaque mois.
Je ne vais pas à Montréal chaque mois.
Est-ce que tu vas à Montréal chaque mois?

S V O

**présent
de l'indicatif**

(Je vais) Je suis en train d'aller à Montréal maintenant.
Je ne suis pas en train d'aller à Montréal maintenant.
Est-ce que tu es en train d'aller à Montréal maintenant?

S V O

**futur
simple**

J'irai à Montréal le mois prochain.
Je n'irai pas à Montréal le mois prochain.
Est-ce que tu iras à Montréal le mois prochain?

S A V O

**futur
en
progrès**

Je serai en train d'aller à Montréal à 17h00 ce soir.
Je ne serai pas en train d'aller à Montréal à 17h00 ce soir.
Seras-tu en train d'aller à Montréal à 17h00 ce soir?

There are 6 *Perfect tenses* in English. There are 4 in French known as *Compound tenses* which equal the 6 *Perfect tenses* in English. These *tenses* in both English and in French are used to state a *duration* or *period of time*.

Conjugating a *Perfect/Compound tense* in English and in French means that you need to combine either the verb *to have/avoir* or *to be/être* followed by the *past participle/* le *participe passé*. The name of the *tense* that you are using reflects the *tense* of the auxiliary verb *to have/avoir* or *to be/être*.

 Note: The English tenses are listed first followed by the French equivalent tense.

Past Perfect plus-que-parfait	I had seen J'avais vu
Past Perfect Continuous imparfait + depuis	I had been waiting J'attendais depuis
Present Perfect passé composé	I have seen J'ai vu
Present Perfect Continuous présent + depuis	I have been waiting J'attends depuis
Future Perfect futur anténieur	I will have seen J'aurai vu
Future Perfect Continuous ça fera + présent	I will have been waiting ça fera...que j'attends

 Note: In English there are *no* exceptions when using the auxiliary *to have* for the conjugation of the *Perfect tenses*. It is always the verb *to have* and *never* the verb *to be*. In French most of the verbs conjugated using the *Compound tenses* are used with the verb *avoir* but there are some exceptions. For a list of exceptions see unit 67.

Past Perfect or *plus-que-parfait* is used to talk about a *duration* of time *up until* a specific time in the past where the speaker stops the *duration* of time by another action.

What is a *duration* of time? A *duration* of time is the *length of time* that has been combined together equaling hours, days, weeks, months or even years.

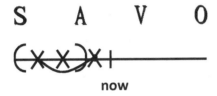

S   A   V   O

now

 I had seen this movie three times before buying it.
J'avais vu ce film trois fois avant de l'acheter.

I had never taken a French course before moving to Québec.
Je n'avais jamais pris un cours de français avant de déménager à Québec.

 The *duration* of time is the key. The action or several actions had taken place *up until* a specific moment in the past that stops the *duration* of time.

 These key words are used to describe a *duration* of time *no later than/pas plus tard que* a specific moment in the past.

before
avant

never
jamais

by

pour = specific time   by noon/pour midi

au = specific date   by May 5th/au 5 mai

en = specific month   by June/en juin
en = specific year   by 2009/en 2009

lorsque ou d'ici à ce que   =   by the time

 Plus-que-parfait = une *durée* de temps *jusqu'à* un moment précis au passé.

The *Past Perfect Continuous* or *imparfait + depuis* is used to talk about a *period* of time in the past that the action had been in *progress up until* a specific time in the past.

What is a *period* of time? A *period* of time explains *how long* an action was, is or *will be in progress.*

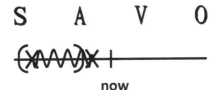

now

It had been raining for 15 minutes when I realized that I had left my clothes on the clothesline.
Il pleuvait depuis 15 minutes quand je me suis rendu compte que j'avais laissé mes vêtements sur la corde à linge.

I had been waiting at the airport for my flight for two hours when they finally cancelled it.
J'attendais à l'aéroport pour mon vol depuis deux heures quand ils l'ont finalement annulé.

I had been driving to Montreal for 45 minutes before I saw an accident.
Je conduisais en direction de Montréal depuis 45 minutes avant que j'aie vu un accident.

I had been walking for 30 minutes before I met my friend.
Je marchais depuis 30 minutes avant que j'aie rencontré mon ami.

The key is the *period* of time that the action had been in *progress* before a second action happened.

Le clé est; la durée de temps qui était en progression avant qu'une autre action soit arrivée.

The *Persent Perfect* or *passé composé* is used to talk about a *duration* of time *up until* the time of speaking. The action or actions are *not* important but the *duration* of time is. We do *not* know when the action(s) happened but the time is *not* over it is *until now/jusqu'à maintenant.*

S   A   V   O

now

Examples:

I have seen this movie three times.
J'ai vu ce film trois fois.

I have never been to Paris.
Je ne suis jamais allé à Paris.

He has already done his homework.
Il a déjà fait ses devoirs.

Exceptions:

Exceptions between English and French using the verbs *to be/être* and *to have/avoir* with since/for/depuis.

I have been sick since Monday.
Je suis malade depuis lundi.

We have been married for 15 years.
Nous sommes mariés depuis 15 ans.

I have had my car for five years.
J'ai mon auto depuis cinq ans.

Note:

The verbs *to be* and *to have* are exceptions when using the *Present Perfect.* In French it is necessary to use the verb *être* ou *avoir* au *présent* + *depuis* to equal the same meaning in English using the *Present Perfect have/has been* meaning *until now.* With the other verbs *passé composé* has the same meaning in French as in English. See examples above.

Key Words:

already	this week	today	in my life	lately
déjà	cette semaine	aujourd'hui	dans ma vie	dernièrement
yet	this month	this year	never	recently
déjà	ce mois-ci	cette année	jamais	récemment
ever	superlatives	number of times	how many times	several times
déjà	superlatifs	nombre de fois	combien de fois	plusieurs fois

Exceptions: With *it is the first time* the *présent de l'indicatif* is used in French as the *Present Perfect* is used in English.

Examples: It is the first time that I have seen this movie.
C'est la première fois que je vois ce film.

The *Present Perfect Continuous or présent + depuis* is used to tell someone *how long* an action has been in *progress up until* the time of speaking. In French it is conjugated with un *verbe* au *présent + depuis* ou "*ça fait* " un temps que.

 An action that started in the past and has been in *progress until now*. La *durée* de temps qui est en *progrèssion jusqu'à maintenant.*

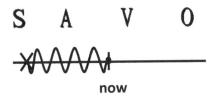

S A V O

now

I have been working here since May. Je travaille ici depuis mai.	I have been waiting here for ten minutes. J'attends ici depuis dix minutes.
She has been working since 8:00am Elle travaille depuis 08h00 ce matin.	I have been playing soccer for one hour. Je joue au soccer depuis une heure.
I have been living here since 2005. Je demeure ici depuis 2005.	I have been learning French for two years. J'apprends le français depuis deux ans.

 There is a difference between "*since and for* " in English, in French it is just "*depuis.* "

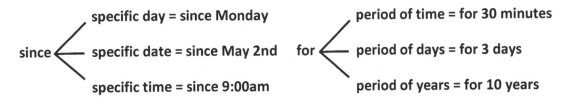

specific day = since Monday   period of time = for 30 minutes

since ⟵ specific date = since May 2nd   for ⟵ period of days = for 3 days

specific time = since 9:00am   period of years = for 10 years

 You cannot move Monday in a week, example: Friday, Wednesday, Sunday, Monday, Saturday, the week follows an order; Monday, Tuesday, Wednesday etc. The same as a month, you cannot move June in a calendar year, example: March, September, June, December etc. the calendar follows an order; January, February, March etc. Therefore the time is *fixed* and *cannot* move so you need to use *since.*

 It is possible to move 30 minutes in a day, example: 30 minutes can be from 8:30am to 9:00am or it can also be from 1:00pm to 1:30pm or from 5:00pm to 5:30pm. The same is possible for weeks and years, you can combine any 3 days or any 5 years together. Therefore the time is *not* fixed and you need to use *for.*

The *Future Perfect* or *futur antérieur* is used to state a *duration* of time that either started in the past or starts from the time of speaking that will be *stopped* in the future by a specific moment. The speaker will stop the *duration* of time in the future by another action or by a specific time.

S   A   V   O

now

Examples: By 9:00pm tonight, I will have taught five English classes.
D'ici 21h00 ce soir, j'aurai enseigné cinq cours d'anglais.

By 2035, I will have paid off my mortgage.
En 2035, j'aurai remboursé toute mon hypothèque.

By October 15th, I will have spent six months in Afghanistan.
Rendu au 15 octobre, j'aurai passé six mois en Afghanistan.

By the time the policeman arrives, the man will have stolen the money.
Lorsque la police arrivera, l'homme aura volé l'argent.

These key words are talking about a *duration* of time *no later than/pas plus tard que* a specific moment in the future.

Key Words:

before avant	pour = specific time	by noon/pour midi
as soon as bien que	**by** au = specific date	by May 5th/au 5 mai
	en = specific month en = specific year	by June/en juin by 2009/en 2009
never jamais	lorsque ou d'ici à ce que = by the time	

Note: *Futur antérieur* = une *durée* de temps *jusqu'à* un moment précis au futur.

Future Perfect Continuous

The *Future Perfect Continuous or ça fera* is used to tell someone *how long* an action will have been in progress by a specific time in the future.

In French there is *no* tense so to conjugate this tense in English you say *ça fera* ou *ça va faire* + le *verbe au présent.*

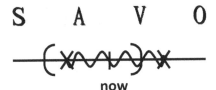

now

 Examples: By November, I will have been working on this project for one year.
En novembre, ça fera un an que je travaille sur ce projet.

By 2023, I will have been living here for ten years.
En 2023, ça fera dix ans que je demeure ici.

By the time the bus arrives, I will have been waiting 30 minutes.
Lorsque l'autobus arrivera, ça fera 30 minutes que j'attends.

By 5:00pm, I will have been working for eight hours.
D'ici 17h00, ça fera huit heures que je travaille.

 Note: The action has been in *progress up until* the time of speaking or starts at the time of speaking and will continue to be in *progress up until* a specific time in the future.

 Note: L'action est en *progression* depuis un temps au passé *jusqu'à* maintenant ou elle commence à ce moment et elle continuera d'être en *progression jusqu'à* un moment précis au futur.

 Note: A *time clause* is used in English when conjugating the *Future Perfect* and *Future Perfect Continuous tenses* when using "*by the time*" in English and "*lorsque*" in French. For examples see unit 68.

Simple Past	Present Perfect
The action here is important.	The *duration* of time is more important than the action(s).
1. An action in the past that is finished.	1. An action in the past that is finished.
2. There is *no* connection to the present.	2. There is a connection to the present.
3. The time is finished.	3. The time is *not* finished.
4. We know when the action happened.	4. We do *not* know when the action happened.
5. The action did *not* happen in a *duration* of time *until now*.	5. The action or actions happened in a *duration* of time *until now*.

Examples:

J'ai fait (je fis) mes devoirs hier.
I did my homework yesterday.

J'ai déjà fait mes devoirs.
I have already done my homework.

Note:

It is impossible to say in French «*j'ai déjà fait mes devoirs hier* » because «*j'ai fait* » is the *duration* of time which means *until now*. You cannot move *now* backwards to finish yesterday, now is now, it cannot move.

Key Words: Key words for Simple Past

Key words for the Present Perfect

ago	lately	already	number of times
when	recently	before	many times
this	yet	this	how many times
yesterday	ever	today	several times
last	never	always	superlatives

Exceptions:

Exceptions with *to be/être* and *to have/avoir* using *Present Perfect see unit 30.*

since/depuis: a specific day; Friday, specific date; May 16th, specific time; 9:00am

for/depuis: a period of time; for 30 minutes, for 3 days, for 5 years

Note: Today can be separated into 3 sections: morning, afternoon and evening. If it is 9:00am on the same day then the *duration* of time is *up until* the time of speaking (now). The morning equals a *duration* of time. Ex: *I have drunk three coffees this morning/j'ai bu trois cafés ce matin.* But if the time is 3:00pm on the same day then the morning is *over*, it is *not up until* the time of speaking. Ex: *I drank a coffee this morning/j'ai bu un café ce matin.* The morning is *over*, it stopped at 12:00pm therefore the *duration* of time is *not up until* the time of speaking (now).

Sentence Structures in English vs. Perfect Tenses

Past
Perfect

S   A   V   O

negative
S **A N** V O
questions
A S V O

Past
Perfect
Continuous

S   A   V   O

negative
S **A N** V O
questions
A S V O

Present
Perfect

S   A   V   O

negative
S **A N** V O
questions
A S V O

Present
Perfect
Continuous

S   A   V   O

negative
S **A N** V O
questions
A S V O

Future
Perfect

S   A   V   O

negative
S **A N** V O
questions
A S V O

Future
Perfect
Continuous

S   A   V   O

negative
S **A N** V O
questions
A S V O

S A V   O

Perfect
Past

I had seen this movie three times before buying it.
I had not seen this movie three times before buying it.
Had you seen this movie three times before buying it?

S A V   V   O

Perfect
Past
Continuous

It had been raining for ten minutes before I went outside.
It had not been raining for ten minutes before I went outside.
Had it been raining for ten minutes before you went outside?

S A V   O

Present
Perfect

I have seen this movie three times.
I have not seen this movie three times.
Have you seen this movie three times?

S A V   V   O

Present
Perfect
Continuous

It has been raining for two hours.
It has not been raining for two hours.
Has it been raining for two hours?

S A V   V   O

Future
Perfect

I will have seen this movie five times by Friday.
I will not have seen this movie five times by Friday.
Will you have seen this movie five times by Friday?

S A V   V   V   O

Future
Perfect
Continuous

It will have been raining for three hours by 5:00pm.
It will not have been raining for three hours by 5:00pm.
Will it have been raining for three hours by 5:00pm?

plus-que-parfait | S | A | V | O

négative
S **NA N** V O
questions
A S V O

imparfait + depuis | S S | A | V V | O O

négative
S **NA N** V O
S **N** V **N** O
questions
A S V O

passé composé | S | A | V | O

négative
S **NA N** V O
questions
A S V O

présent + depuis | S S | A | V V | O O

négative
S **NA N** V O
S **N** V **N** O
questions
A S V O

futur antérieur | S | A | V | O

négative
S **NA N** V O
questions
A S V O

ça fera + verbe au présent | S | | V | O

négative
S **N** V **N** O
questions
A S V O

S A V O

plus-que-
parfait

J'avais vu ce film trois fois avant de l'acheter.
Je n'avais pas vu ce film trois fois avant de l'acheter.
Avais- tu vu ce film trois fois avant de l'acheter?

S V O

imparfait +
depuis

Il pleuvait depuis dix minutes quand je suis allé dehors.
Il ne pleuvait pas depuis dix minutes quand je suis allé dehors.
Est-ce qu'il pleuvait depuis dix minutes quand tu es allé dehors?

S A V O

passé
composé

J'ai vu ce film trois fois.
Je n'ai pas vu ce film trois fois.
As-tu vu ce film trois fois?

S V O

présent +
depuis

Il pleut depuis deux heures.
Il ne pleut pas depuis deux heures.
Est-ce qu'il pleut depuis deux heures?

S A V O

futur
antérieur

J'aurai vu ce film cinq fois d'ici vendredi.
Je n'aurai pas vu ce film cinq fois d'ici vendredi.
Auras-tu vu ce film cinq fois d'ici vendredi?

S V O

ça fera +
verbe au présent

D'ici 17h00 ce soir, ça fera trois heures qu'il pleut.
D'ici 17h00 ce soir, ça ne fera pas trois heures qu'il pleut.
D'ici 17h00 ce soir, est-ce que ça fera trois heures qu'il pleut?

Time Lines

Simple Past

now

Past Continuous

now

Simple Present

now

Present Continuous

now

Simple Future

now

Future Continuous

now

Past Perfect

now

Past Perfect Continuous

now

Present Perfect

?

now

Present Perfect Continuous

now

Future Perfect

now

Future Perfect Continuous

now

Auxiliaries

_____

Modal Auxiliaries are used to specify a mood or voice, willingness and or capability.

There are many *auxiliaries* in English as well as in French. In French see the verbs "*pouvoir* " and "*devoir.* "

Examples:

can	peut
could	pouvait/savait/pourrait
may	peut-être
might	peut-être
should	devrait
ought to	devrait
have to	doit
have got to	doit
must	doit/il faut que
will	rai, ras, ra, rons, rez, ront
would	rais, rais, rait, rions, riez, raient
had better	ferait mieux

Note:

All *auxiliaries* are followed by the *base form* in English and by the *infinitive* in French. For the difference between the *infinitive* and *base forms* of the verbs see unit 57.

	Affirmative SAVO	Negative SANVO	Questions ASVO	Past Tense SAVO
Can:	I can swim. Je peux nager.	I cannot swim. Je ne peux pas nager.	Can you swim? Peux-tu nager?	I could swim when I was 3. Je pouvais/savais nager quand j'avais trois ans.
	an ability	an inability	to question an ability	past ability or knowledge
Could:	I could do that for you. Je pourrais faire ça pour vous.	I couldn't be a doctor. Je ne pourrais pas être un médecin.	Could you help me? Pourriez-vous m'aider?	I could have seen that show if I had been there. J'aurais pu voir le spectacle si j'avais été là.
	I could do that if I had time. Je pourrais farie ça si j'avais le temps.	I couldn't work last week. Je n'ai pas pu ou je ne pouvais pas...		
	present/future possibility	present/past impossibility or past inability	to question a possibility	past possibility
May:	It may rain tomorrow. Il va peut-être pleuvoir demain.	It may not rain. Il ne va peut-être pas pleuvoir.	May I speak with John? Puis-je parler avec John?	I may have given him the letter. Je lui ai peut-être donné la lettre.
	50% possibility	50% possibility	polite question	50% past possibility
Might:	It might snow tomorrow. Il va peut-être neiger demain.	It might not snow. Il ne va peut-être pas neiger.		I might have made a mistake. J'ai peut-être fait une erreur.
	50% possibility	50% possibility		50 % past possibility

Can is used to talk about an *ability* both in English and in French. When using *can* as a question it is *not* a polite question to ask unless you are trying to find if someone is *capable* of doing something. If you replace *can* with *able to* you will have the exact meaning to the statements or questions you would like to make or ask.

Affirmative	Negative	Questions	Past Tense
I can	I cannot	Can I...?	I could
You can	You cannot	Can you...?	You could
He can	He cannot	Can he...?	He could
We can	We cannot	Can we...?	We could
You can	You cannot	Can you...?	You could
They can	They cannot	Can they...?	They could
Je peux	Je ne peux pas	Est-ce je peux...?	Je pouvais/savais
Tu peux	Tu ne peux pas	Peux-tu...?	Tu pouvais/savais
Il peut	Il ne peut pas	Peut-il...?	Il pouvait/savait
Nous pouvons	Nous ne pouvons pas	Pouvons- nous...?	Nous pouvions/savions
Vous pouvez	Vous ne pouvez pas	Pouvez-vous...?	Vous pouviez/saviez
Ils peuvent	Ils ne peuvent pas	Peuvent-ils...?	Ils pouvaient/savaient

 The past of *can* is "*could.*" It states the *past ability* of the speaker meaning that the person "*was able to/était capable*" or "*knew how to/savait.*"

 After *auxiliaries* in English you need to use the *base form* of a verb *not* the *Present tense* of a verb. See examples below.

 In French however after the auxiliary *pouvoir* you need to use *l'infinitif* which equals the *base form* of a verb in English. For the differences between the *infinitive* and *base forms* of a verb see unit 57.

	Correct	Incorrect	Incorrect
Examples:	I can swim.	I can to swim.	He can swims.
	Je peux nager.	Je peux nage.	Il peut nage.

84

Could is used to talk about a *possibility* both in English and in French. A *possibility* using *could* is a chance of *success* more or less than 33% but *not* more than 50%.

Affirmative	Negative	Questions	Past Tense
I could	I could not	Could I ...?	I could have done
You could	You could not	Could you...?	You could have done
He could	He could not	Could he...?	He could have done
We could	We could not	Could we...?	We could have done
You could	You could not	Could you...?	You could have done
They could	They could not	Could they...?	They could have done

Je pourrais	Je n'ai pas pu	Pourrais-je...?	J'aurais pu faire
Tu pourrais	Tu n'as pas pu	Pourrais -tu...?	Tu aurais pu faire
Il pourrait	Il n'a pas pu	Pourrait-il ...?	Il aurait pu faire
Nous pourrions	Nous n'avons pas pu	Pourrions -nous...?	Nous aurions pu faire
Vous pourriez	Vous n'avez pas pu	Pourriez -vous...?	Vous auriez pu faire
Ils pourraient	Ils n'ont pas pu	Pourraient-ils...?	Ils auraient pu faire

The *Present tense* of *could* means that it is a *possibility now* or in the *near future.*
C'est possible *maintenant* ou *bientôt.* The future meaning of *could* is *conditional*
meaning that for the action to be a *possibility* you need the *condition* to happen first.
"It would be possible if/Il serait possible si. "

I could do it for you.
Je pourrais le faire pour vous.

I could buy a house if I won the lottery.
Je pourrais acheter une maison si je
gagnais à la loterie.

In English the *Past tense* of *could* is conjugated with the auxiliary *could* followed by
the *base form* of the verb *to have* plus the *past participle.*
In French however you need to use the *conditionnel présent* of the verb *avoir* plus le
participe passé of the auxiliary *pouvoir* followed by *l'infinitif.*

I could have done my homework Monday.
J'aurais pu faire mes devoirs lundi.

The *contraction* for the *Past tense* in English is also used in speaking and in writing
whereas the slang is used *only* for speaking.

Contraction
I could've done my homework Monday.

Slang
I coulda done my homework Monday.

<table>
<tr><td>Unit
44</td><td>May</td></tr>
</table>

May is used to talk about a 50% chance that something is *possible* in the *present* or *near future*.

Affirmative	Negative	Questions	Past Tense
I may	I may not	May I ...?	I may have seen
You may	You may not		You may have seen
He may	He may not		He may have seen
We may	We may not	May we...?	We may have seen
You may	You may not		You may have seen
They may	They may not		They may have seen
Je vais peut-être	Je ne vais peut-être pas	Puis-je...?	J'ai peut-être vu
Tu vas peut-être	Tu ne vas peut-être pas		Tu as peut-être vu
Il va peut-être	Il ne va peut-être pas		Il a peut-être vu
Nous allons peut-être	Nous n'allons peut-être...	Puissions-nous...?	Nous avons peut-être..
Vous allez peut-être	Vous n'allez peut-être pas		Vous avez peut-être...
Ils vont peut-être	Ils ne vont peut-être pas		Ils ont peut-être vu

 Questions using *may* in English and French are 1st person singular and plural *only*.

All auxiliaries are followed by the *base form* in English and by the *infinitive* in French.

 In English the *Past tense* of *may* is the auxiliary *may* followed by the *base form* of the verb *to have* plus the *past participle*.

In French the *Past tense* is conjugated with the verbs *avoir* ou *être* au présent followed by "*peut-être*" plus le *participe passé*.

 I may have forgotten my keys at work.
J'ai peut-être oublié mes clés au travail.

He may have gone to the movies last night.
Il est peut-être allé au cinéma hier soir.

 For a list of verbs used with the auxiliary *être* see unit 67.

Might is used to talk about a 50% chance that something is *possible* in the *present* or *near future.* It is used the same way as *may.*

Affirmative	Negative	Questions	Past Tense
I might	I might not		I might have gone
You might	You might not		You might have gone
He might	He might not		He might have gone
We might	We might not		We might have gone
You might	You might not		You might have gone
They might	They might not		They might have gone

Je vais peut-être	Je ne vais peut-être pas		Je suis peut-être allé
Tu vas peut-être	Tu ne vas peut-être pas		Tu es peut-être allé
Il va peut-être	Il ne va peut-être pas		Il est peut-être allé
Nous allons peut-être	Nous n'allons peut-être pas		Nous sommes peut-être…
Vous allez peut-être	Vous n'allez peut-être pas		Vous êtes peut-être allés
Ils vont peut-être	Ils ne vont peut-être pas		Ils sont peut-être allés

 Questions using *might* in English are rarely used as it is old English. *May* is much more common with the same meaning.

All *auxiliaries* are followed by the *base form* in English and by the *infinitive* in French.

 In English the *Past tense* of *might* is conjugated with the auxiliary *might* followed by the *base form* of the verb *to have* plus the *past participle.*

In French the *Past tense* of *might* is conjugated with the verbs *avoir* ou *être* au *présent* followed by "*peut-être*" plus le *participe passé.*

 I might have seen this movie last year.
J'ai peut-être vu ce film l'année passée.

I might have given her the wrong information.
Je lui ai peut-être donné les mauvaises informations.

 For a list of verbs used with the auxiliary *être* see unit 67.

For a list of verbs used with the auxiliary *être* see unit 67.

90

	Affirmative SAVO	Negative SANVO	Questions ASVO	Past Tense SAVO
Should:	I should do my homework. Je devrais faire mes devoirs.	I should not do my homework. Je ne devrais pas faire mes devoirs.	Should I do my homework? Devrais-je faire mes devoirs?	I should have done my homework last Monday. J'aurais dû faire mes devoirs lundi passé.
	90% suggestion or expectation	90% restraint	to question a suggestion or expectation	past suggestion or expectation or regret
Have to:	I have to work tomorrow. Je dois travailler demain.	I do not have to work tomorrow. Je ne dois pas travailler demain.	Do you have to work tomorrow? Est-ce que tu dois travailler demain?	I had to work Monday. J'ai dû travailler lundi.
	100% obligation	0% obligation	to question an obligation	100% past obligation
Must:	He must be Il doit être Il faut qu'il soit	He must not be Il ne doit pas être Il ne faut pas que	Why must he be...? Pourquoi doit-il...? Pourquoi faut-il...?	He must have been there. Il a sûrement été là. Il faut qu'il ait été là.
	95% obligation	95% forbidden	to question an obligation	95% past belief

Note: There are two reasons for using *must* listed below.

1. *Must* = a 95 % obligation. *Must* is a requirement or fulfilment being *obliged* to do something. It is not an order so using *must* gives you a bit of a choice to do the action if you do *not* do the action there could be consequences.

2. *Must* = something believed to be true by 95% certainty.

Should or *ought to* is used to talk about a *suggestion* or *probability* both in English and French. A *suggestion* is something you would like to see done by 90% meaning it is *not* quite an *order* at 100% like you *have to.* It is used more as a *recommendation* then an *order.*

Affirmative	Negative	Questions	Past Tense
I should	I should not	Should I...?	I should have seen
You should	You should not	Should you...?	You should have seen
He should	He should not	Should he...?	He should have seen
We should	We should not	Should we...?	We should have seen
You should	You should not	Should you...?	You should have seen
They should	They should not	Should they...?	They should have seen
Je devrais	Je ne devrais pas	Devrais- je...?	J'aurais dû voir
Tu devrais	Tu ne devrais pas	Devrais -tu...?	Tu aurais dû voir
Il devrait	Il ne devrait pas	Devrait-il...?	Il aurait dû voir
Nous devrions	Nous ne devrions pas	Devrions- nous...?	Nous aurions dû voir
Vous devriez	Vous ne devriez pas	Devriez-vous...?	Vous auriez dû voir
Ils devraient	Ils ne devraient pas	Devraient-ils...?	Ils auraient dû voir

 Note: All *auxiliaries* are followed by the *base form* in English and by the *infinitive* in French.

 Note: In English the *Past tense* of *should* is conjugated with the auxiliary *should* followed by the *base form* of the verb *to have* plus the *past participle.*

In French the *Past tense* of *should* is conjugated with the verb *avoir* used in the *conditionnel présent* plus le *participe passé* of the verb *devoir* followed by *l'infinitif.*

 Examples: I should have seen that movie in the theatre last year.
J'aurais dû voir ce film au théâtre l'année passée.

We should have taken more pictures.
Nous aurions dû prendre plus de photos.

 Note: *Ought to* can also be used instead of *should* although it is *not* as common.

Have to or *have got to* are used to talk about a 100% *obligation* both in English and in French. It is something that you do *not* have a *choice* to do.

Affirmative	Negative	Questions	Past Tense
I have to	I do not have to	Do I have to...?	I had to go
You have to	You do not have to	Do you have to...?	You had to go
He has to	He does not have to	Does he have to...?	He had to go
We have to	We do not have to	Do we have to...?	We had to go
You have to	You do not have to	Do you have to...?	You had to go
They have to	They do not have to	Do they have to...?	They had to go

Je dois	Je ne dois pas	Est-ce que je dois...?	J'ai dû aller
Tu dois	Tu ne dois pas	Est-ce que tu dois...?	Tu as dû aller
Il doit	Il ne doit pas	Est-ce qu'il doit...?	Il a dû aller
Nous devons	Nous ne devons pas	Est-ce que nous devons..?	Nous avons dû aller
Vous devez	Vous ne devez pas	Est-ce que vous devez..?	Vous avez dû aller
Ils doivent	Ils ne doivent pas	Est-ce qu'ils doivent..?	Ils ont dû aller

 Note: All auxiliaries are followed by the *base form* in English and by the *infinitive* in French.

 Note: In English the *Past tense* of *have to* is conjugated using *had to* followed by the *base form* of a verb.

In French the *Past tense of have to* is conjugated using *avoir* au *présent* plus le *participe passé* of the verb *devoir* followed by *l'infinitif*.

 Examples: I had to work yesterday.
J'ai dû travailler hier.

 Note: *Have to* or *have got to* are used more as a *personal obligation* than *must*. You "*have to* " comes across as an *order* when speaking to someone else.

Must is used to talk about a 95% *obligation* both in English and in French. It is more *business oriented* meaning that you have a bit of a *choice* to do the action or *not*. Another reason for using *must* is if you believe something is true.

Affirmative	Negative	Questions	Past Tense
I must	I must not	Must I...?	I must have done
You must	You must not	Must you...?	You must have done
He must	He must not	Must he...?	He must have done
We must	We must not	Must we...?	We must have done
You must	You must not	Must you...?	You must have done
They must	They must not	Must they...?	They must have done
Il faut que je	Il ne faut pas que je	Faut-il ...?	Il faut que j'aie fait
Il faut que tu	Il ne faut pas que tu	Faut-il ...?	Il faut que tu aies fait
Il faut qu'il	Il ne faut pas qu'il	Faut-il ...?	Il faut qu'il ait fait
Il faut que nous	Il ne faut pas que nous	Faut-il ...?	Il faut que nous ayons fait
Il faut que vous	Il ne faut pas que vous	Faut-il ...?	Il faut que vous ayez fait
Il faut qu'ils	Il ne faut pas qu'ils	Faut-il ...?	Il faut qu'ils aient fait
Je dois	Je ne dois pas	Dois-je...?	J'ai dû sûrement
Tu dois	Tu ne dois pas	Dois-tu...?	Tu as dû sûrement
Il doit	Il ne doit pas	Doit-il...?	Il a dû sûrement
Nous devons	Nous ne devons pas	Devons-nous...?	Nous avons dû sûrement
Vous devez	Vous ne devez pas	Devez-vous...?	Vous avez dû sûrement
Ils doivent	Ils ne doivent pas	Doivent-ils...?	Ils ont dû sûrement

 Note: In French both *il faut que* as well as *doit* are used to mean a 95% *obligation*. With the verb "*falloir/il faut que* " in French the *subjoncitif* is used and *not* the *base form* of the verb as in English.

The *Past tense* of "*il faut que* " is followed by le *présent du subjonctif* of the verb *avoir* ou *être* followed by le *participe passé*. When the verb *être* is used to conjugate the *Past tense* of *il faut que*, it is used as the auxiliary only with *les verbes pronominaux* and some *exception* verbs. For a list of the *exception* verbs see unit 67.

 Note: *Pronominal verbs* are *verbs* in French which need a *reflexive pronoun* in addition to a *subject pronoun* because the *subject* performing the action has the same action being acted upon as the *object*.

 Examples:

To get up	Se lever
I got up at 7:00am this morning.	Je me suis levé à 07h00 ce matin.

	Affirmative SVVO/SAVO	Negative SANVO	Questions ASVO	Past Tense SAVO
Want:	I want to go to Florida. Je veux aller en Floride.	I do not want to go to Florida. Je ne veux pas aller en Floride.	Do you want to go to Florida? Veux-tu aller en Floride?	I wanted to go to Florida last year. Je voulais aller en Floride l'année passée. J'ai voulu aller...
	a desire	lack of desire	to question a desire	past desire
Would like:	I would like to learn English. J'aimerais apprendre l'anglais.	I would not like to learn English. Je n'aimerais pas apprendre l'anglais.	Would you like to learn English? Aimeriez-vous...? Souhaiteriez-vous...? Voudriez-vous...?	I would have liked to learn English eariler. J'aurais aimé apprendre l'anglais plus tôt.
	polite desire	polite lack of desire	to question a desire	past polite desire
Would:	I would join the Army. Je m'engagerais dans l'armée.	I would not join the Army. Je ne m'engagerais pas dans l'armée.	Would you join the Army? Vous engageriez-vous dans l'armée?	I would have joined if I were younger. Je me serais engagé dans l'armée si j'étais plus jeune.
	condition required or needed	lack of a condition or need	to question a condition or need	past condition required or needed

Note: In French the verbs *vouloir, desirer* and *souhaiter* can be used as a polite *desire.* The conjugation of the verb *vouloir* in the *Present tense* using *veut/want* is *not* a polite *desire* in English and in French. When using any other verb in the *Conditional tense* it means that the verb has a *condition* attached to it. See unit 71.

Personal Notes

Want is a *desire* to have something that is *missing* or *lacking*.

Affirmative	Negative	Questions	Past Tense
I want to go	I do not want to go	Do I want...?	I wanted to go
You want to go	You do not want to go	Do you want...?	You wanted to go
He wants to go	He does not want to go	Does he want...?	He wanted to go
We want to go	We do not want to go	Do we want...?	We wanted to go
You want to go	You do not want to go	Do you want...?	You wanted to go
They want to go	They do not want to go	Do they want...?	They wanted to go

Je veux aller	Je ne veux pas aller	Est-ce que je veux...?	Je voulais aller
Tu veux aller	Tu ne veux pas aller	Veux-tu...?	Tu voulais aller
Il veut aller	Il ne veut pas aller	Veut-il...?	Il voulait aller
Nous voulons aller	Nous ne voulons pas aller	Voulons-nous...?	Nous voulions aller
Vous voulez aller	Vous ne voulez pas aller	Voulez-vous...?	Vous vouliez aller
Ils veulent aller	Ils ne veulent pas aller	Veulent-ils...?	Ils voulaient aller

 Note: In French the conjugation of the verb *vouloir* in the *Present tense* and the *Past tense* is followed by an *infinitive form* of a verb.

When using *imparfait* as the *Past tense* of *vouloir* there needs to be another action happen at the same time in the past to equal the *Simple Past tense* in English. If there was *no* other action happening at the same time you need to use *passé composé* which still equals the *Simple Past tense* in English. See examples below.

 Examples: I wanted to learn English when I was young.
Je voulais apprendre l'anglais quand j'étais jeune.

I wanted to go to the movies last night.
J'ai voulu aller au cinéma hier soir.

 Note: To *want* something is *not* a polite way of stating a *desire* or *wish*. There is a better way of stating or asking a *desire* which is *would like/aimerait* both in English and in French.

Would like is a polite *desire* stating that something is *missing* or *lacking*. In French use the *conditionnel présent* of the verbs *aimer* ou *vouloir* to state a polite *desire*.

Affirmative	Negative	Questions	Past Tense
I would like	I would not like	Would I like...?	I would have liked
You would like	You would not like	Would you like...?	You would have liked
He would like	He would not like	Would he like...?	He would have liked
We would like	We would not like	Would we like...?	We would have liked
You would like	You would not like	Would you like...?	You would have liked
They would like	They would not like	Would they like...?	They would have liked
J'aimerais	Je n'aimerais pas	Aimerais-je...?	J'aurais aimé
Tu aimerais	Tu n'aimerais pas	Aimerais-tu...?	Tu aurais aimé
Il aimerait	Il n'aimerait pas	Aimerait-il...?	Il aurait aimé
Nous aimerions	Nous n'aimerions pas	Aimerions-nous...?	Nous aurions aimé
Vous aimeriez	Vous n'aimeriez pas	Aimeriez-vous...?	Vous auriez aimé
Ils aimeraient	Ils n'aimeraient pas	Aimeraient-ils...?	Ils auraient aimé
Je voudrais	Je ne voudrais pas	Voudrais-je...?	J'aurais voulu
Tu voudrais	Tu ne voudrais pas	Voudrais-tu...?	Tu aurais voulu
Il voudrait	Il ne voudrait pas	Voudrait-il...?	Il aurait voulu
Nous voudrions	Nous ne voudrions pas	Voudrions nous...?	Nous aurions voulu
Vous voudriez	Vous ne voudriez pas	Voudriez vous...?	Vous auriez voulu
Ils voudraient	Ils ne voudraient pas	Voudraient-ils...?	Ils auraient voulu

 You can also use the verb *desirer* in French in the *conditionnel présent* to state a *desire* that is *missing* or *lacking*.

In English the *Past Conditional tense* is used with *would have* followed by the *past participle*.

 In French the *conditionnel passé* is conjugated using the *conditionnel présent* of *avoir* ou *être* followed by le *participe passé*.

When the verb "*être* " is used to conjugate the *conditionnel passé* it is used as the auxiliary *only* with les *verbes pronominaux* and some *exception* verbs. See unit 67 for a list of the *exception* verbs.

Conditional tenses talk about a verb that has a condition attached to it. In order to have the first action happen either in the past, present or future the condition needs to happen first.

Affirmative	Negative	Questions	Past Tense
I would do	I would not go	Would I eat...?	I would have done
You would do	You would not go	Would you eat...?	You would have done
He would do	He would not go	Would he eat...?	He would have done
We would do	We would not go	Would we eat...?	We would have done
You would do	You would not go	Would you eat...?	You would have done
They would do	They would not go	Would they eat...?	They would have done
Je ferais	Je n'irais pas	Mangerais-je...?	J'aurais fait
Tu ferais	Tu n'irais pas	Mangerais-tu...?	Tu aurais fait
Il ferait	Il n'irait pas	Mangerait-il...?	Il aurait fait
Nous ferions	Nous n'irions pas	Mangerions-nous...?	Nous aurions fait
Vous feriez	Vous n'iriez pas	Mangeriez-vous...?	Vous auriez fait
Ils feraient	Ils n'iraient pas	Mangeraient-ils...?	Ils auraient fait

 In English and in French this tense is known as *Conditional Present.* In French note that each verb ending changes with each *subject.* In English however you just put the auxiliary *would* in front of the *base form* of a verb to conjugate it to a *Conditional tense.*

 In English the *Past Conditional tense* is used with *would have* followed by the *past participle.*

In French the *conditionnel passé* is used with the *conditionnel présent* of *avoir* ou *être* followed by le *participe passé.*

Examples:

I would have seen	J'aurais vu	I would have gone	Je serais allé
You would have seen	Tu aurais vu	You would have gone	Tu serais allé
He would have seen	Il aurait vu	He would have gone	Il serait allé
We would have seen	Nous aurions vu	We would have gone	Nous serions allés
You would have seen	Vous auriez vu	You would have gone	Vous seriez allés
They would have seen	Ils auraient vu	They would have gone	Ils seraient allés

 When using the verb *être* in French as the auxiliary to conjugate the *conditionnel passé* the verb *être* is the *exception* to the rule. Normally the verb *avoir* is used followed by le *participe passé.* For a list of the *exception* verbs see unit 67.

Comparisons are used to speak about two objects or two situations that have *likeness* or *similarity*. In English the rules are a lot more complicated than in French. In French it does *not* matter what adjective or adverb you use to compare it to something else you just use "*plus*" before an adjective.

In English it depends on the syllable or syllables of the adjective. If the adjective has one syllable add "*er.*" If the 2 syllable adjective finishes with a "*y*" change the "*y*" to "*ier.*" If the 2 syllable adjective has a soft ending use "*er*"and if it has a hard ending use "*more.*"If the adjective has 3 or more syllables use "*more.*"

1 Syllable	2 Syllables	2 Syllables	2 Syllables	3,4,5 Syllables
plus = «er»	plus = «er»	plus = «er»	plus = «more»	plus = «more»
big/bigger	easy/easier	quiet/quieter	crowded	important
old/older	funny/funnier	gentle/gentler	modern	comfortable
thin/thinner	lucky/luckier	simple/simpler	patient	expensive
large/larger	heavy/heavier	narrow/narrower	pleasant	argumentative
new/newer	pretty/prettier			generous
neat/neater	busy/busier			

The spelling rules for a 1 syllable adjective are as follows: If the adjective finishes with a vowel and a consonant then you double the last letter and add "*er*" example: bigger. If it finishes with a "*w*" then do *not* double the last letter, example: newer. If there are 2 vowels then a consonant you do *not* double the last letter you just add "*er*"example: neater. If it finishes with 2 consonants then just add "*er*" example: taller. If the adjective finishes with an "*e*" then just add "r" example: larger.

When using a 2 syllable adjective that finishes with a "*y*" change the "*y*" to "*i*" and add "*er.*" The 2 syllable adjectives that you use with an "*er*" ending are when the last letters are silent or *soft* making it easy to add "*er.*" When the 2 syllable adjective has a *hard* ending and you hear the last letter it is used with "*more.*" See examples below.

When *narrow* is said the "*w*" is *not* heard therefore use "*er.*"
When *crowded* is said the "*d*" is heard therefore use "*more.*"

Superlatives are the greatest form of an adjective or adverb which tells that something has a greater degree than anything that it is being compared to.

In English use the same rules as *comparisons* only using "*est*" instead of using "*er.*"
In French it does *not* matter what adjective or adverb you use to state the *superlative form* you just use "*le plus*" before the adjective or adverb.

 Note: In English it depends on the syllable or syllables of the adjective. See unit 54 for the rules for comparisons.

Examples:

1 Syllable	2 Syllables	2 Syllables	2 Syllables	3,4,5 Syllables
le plus = «est»	le plus = «est»	le plus = «est»	le plus = «the most»	le plus = «the most»
big/biggest	easy/easiest	quiet/quietest	modern	serious
small/smallest	busy/busiest	narrow/narrowest	crowded	comfortable
thin/thinnest	lucky/luckiest	simple/simplest	patient	expensive
large/largest	funny/funniest	gentle/gentlest	pleasant	important
new/newest	heavy/heaviest			generous
old/oldest	pretty/prettiest			argumentative

 Note: To help you use *comparisons* or *superlatives* correctly note that "*better*" is a comparison finishing with "*er*" and "*the best*" is the top form of the adjective finishing with "*est.*" As a result the conjugation of a *comparison* is "*er*" and the conjugation of a *superlative* is "*est.*"

Examples:

The conjugation of a *comparison*.   The conjugation of a *superlative*.

Better use the ending "*er*"   Best use the ending "*est*"

Big = Bigger   Big = Biggest

good/bon
well/bien better/ meilleur the best/le meilleur

bad/mauvais
badly/mal worse/pire the worst/le pire

far farther/plus loin
further/plus loin the farthest/le plus loin
the furthest/le plus loin

Note: *Further* has a *double signification.* It also means "*more/plus*" when used with *information.*

Examples: May I have further information please?
Puis-je avoir de plus amples informations s'il vous plaît?

Note: In English to change an adjective to an adverb add "*ly*" in French use "*ment.*" To use an adverb in a *comparison form* just use "*more*" in front of the adverb.

Examples: Could you drive more slowly please?
Pourriez-vous conduire plus lentement s'il vous plaît?

Exceptions: There is an exception to using "*more*" with an adverb which is "*early.*" You need to change the "*y*" to "*ier*" or "*y*" to "*iest*" if you want to state a *comparison* or *a superlative form.*

Examples:

early/tôt earlier/plus tôt the earliest/le plus tôt

Exceptions: If you use "*hard*" as an adverb "*hardly*" in English the meaning changes to "*presque jamais* ou *à peine.*"

If you use "*late*" as an adverb "*lately*" in English the meaning changes to "*dernièrement.*"

Note: The following are both adjectives and adverbs that do *not* need to change using "*ly*" or "*ment*" in English and in French.

fast/vite	hard/dur	late/tard
He is fast.	The exam is hard.	It is late.
Il est vite.	L'examen est dur.	C'est tard.
He runs fast.	He does not work hard.	I get up late often.
Il court vite.	Il ne travaille pas dur.	Je me lève tard souvent.

Examples:

Infinitive	Base	Present	Past	Past Participle	Present Participle
to be être	be être	am/are/is suis/est	was/were étais/était	been été	being étant
to do faire	do faire	do/does fais/fait	did fis/fit	done fait	doing faisant
to drink boire	drink boire	drink/drinks bois/boit	drank bus/but	drunk bu	drinking buvant
to drive conduire	drive conduire	drive/drives conduis	drove conduisis	driven conduit	driving conduisant
to eat manger	eat manger	eat/eats mange	ate mangeai	eaten mangé	eating mangeant
to go aller	go aller	go/goes vais/va	went allai	gone allé (e) (s)	going allant
to see voir	see voir	see/sees vois/voit	saw vis/vit	seen vu	seeing voyant
to work travailler	work travailler	work/works travaille	worked travaillai	worked travaillé	working travaillant

 Note: All the verbs in English and in French can be set up in a chart like this one even if they are considered *regular verbs* in English.

 Note: A list of *irregular verbs* in English is at the back of this book see appendices 1-5, if the verb is *not* listed on this list then it is considered a *regular verb* .

The *infinitive form* of the verb is the "*raw form*" of the verb *without* any conjugation. In French *l'infinitif* is used as the *infinitive* and as the *base forms* in English. There is *no base form* of the verb in French so the *infinitive* and the *base forms* are the same. There are different ways of using the *infinitive form* of the verb. See examples below.

1. The *infinitive form* of the verb is used after and already conjugated verb.

I want to go to Florida.
Je veux aller en Floride.

I would like to be a singer.
J'aimerais être un chanteur/une chanteuse.

2. The *infinitive form* is also used in French with "*pour + le verbe infinitif*" to equal the English *infinitive.*

I have a job to pay my bills.
J'ai un emploi pour payer mes factures.

I need a knife to cut my meat.
J'ai besoin d'un couteau pour couper ma viande.

3. It is also possible to use "*de* ou *d'* " in front of "*le verbe infinitif*" in French to equal the English *infinitive.*

There is a better way to travel.
Il y a une meilleure façon de voyager.

4. It is also possible to use "*à* " with "*le verbe infinitif* " in French to equal the English *infinitive.*

I have a lot of things to do today.
J'ai beaucoup de choses à faire aujourd'hui.

There are 4 ways in English to use the *base form* of a verb. The *base form* of a verb is the "*infinitive*" without the "*to.*" The *infinitive* and *base forms* of the verbs are the same in French.

<table>
<tr><td>Infinitive</td><td>Base</td></tr>
</table>

 Examples:

To be   be

être   être

1. The *base form* of the verb is used when we want to conjugate the "*Continuous tenses*" in English and in French using "*en train de.*"

Note: The formula to conjugate the *Continuous tenses* is:

To be	être
+	+
base form	en train de
+	+
ING	le verbe infinitif

2. The *base form* of the verb is used after "*Modal Auxiliaires.*" For *Modal Auxiliaries* see unit 40.

 Examples:

I can swim   Je peux nager

3. The *base form* is also used with the "*Subjunctives*" in English. The *base form* is *not* used with the *Subjunctive tenses* in French, there are 4 *Subjunctive tenses* used instead; *présent du subjonctif, imparfait du subjonctif, passé du subjonctif et plus-que-parfait du subjonctif.*

Correct	Incorrect

 Examples:

I suggested that he do his homework.	I suggested that he does his homework.
J'ai suggéré qu'il fasse ses devoirs.	J'ai suggéré qu'il fait ses devoirs.

4. The *base form* of the verbs can also be used as the "*Imperative tense.*" In English and in French it is considered an *order.* In French this tense can be found at the bottom of a «*Bescherelle*» titled *impératif.*

 Examples:

Eat your vegetables.	Mange tes legumes.
Let's do our homework here.	Faisons nos devoirs ici.
Work harder.	Travaillez plus dur.

There are 2 reasons the *past participle* exists.

1. The *past participle* is to conjugate the *Perfect tenses* in English and the *Compound tenses* in French.

I had eaten	J'avais mangé
I have eaten	J'ai mangé
He has eaten	Il a mangé
I will have eaten	J'aurai mangé
I would have eaten	J'aurais mangé

2. The *past participle* can also be used as an adjective.

Don't sit on this chair. It is broken.
Ne t'asseois pas sur cette chaise. Elle est brisée.

In the example above the verb is "*to be/être* " and the *past participle* is the adjective.

When using the *past participle* as an adjective in French you need to correspond the *past participle* to the *object* in the sentence by adding an "*e* " or "*s* " or "*es* " depending on if the *object* is masculin or féminin, masculin pluriel or féminin pluriel. For examples see unit 62.

Present	Past	Past Participle
break/breaks	broke	broken
brise	brisa	brisé (e) (s)

It is *not* possible to use the *Present tense, Past tense* or the *infinitive form* of a verb as an adjective. See examples below.

The chair is break.	La chaise est brise.
The chair is broke.	La chaise est brisa.
The chair is to break.	La chaise est briser.

There are 3 reasons in English and 2 reasons in French the *present participle* exists.

1. The *present participle* can be used as an adjective.

 Examples:

Working ten hours a day is tiring.	This course is interesting.
Travailler dix heures par jour est fatigant.	Ce cours est intéressant.
I heard some surprising news yesterday.	Water is hydrating.
J'ai entendu des nouvelles surprenantes.	L'eau est hydratante.

2. The *present participle* can also be used as an activity.

 Examples:

While eating, the phone rang.	While reading, I learnt a new word.
En mangeant, le téléphone a sonné.	En lisant, j'ai appris un nouveau mot.
While playing, my son broke his leg.	While working, I received a call.
En jouant, mon fils s'est cassé la jambe.	En travaillant, j'ai reçu un appel.

3. The *present participle* can also be used as a gerund.

 Note: A *gerund* is the *present participle* used as a *subject* or *object* of a sentence. In French un *gérondif* is "*le verbe infinitif* " used as a *sujet* ou *objet* of a sentence.

 Examples:

Thinking in a second language is hard.	Eating is necessary to live.
Penser en une deuxième langue est dur.	Manger est nécessaire pour vivre.
Watching a movie is relaxing.	Playing soccer is fun.
Écouter un film est relaxant.	Jouer au soccer est amusant.
Driving in the winter is more difficult.	Reading is important.
Conduire en hiver est plus difficile.	Lire est important.

 Note: Again, when using the *present participle* as an adjective in French you need to correspond *present participle* to the *object* in the sentence by adding an "*e* " or "*s* " or "*es* "depending on if the *object* is masculin or féminin, masculin pluriel or féminin pluriel. For examples see unit 62.

Personal Notes

123

Active and *Passive tenses* are used to state what is more important in the sentence. Is it the person who did, does, or will do the action that is important or is it the *object* that is more important to the speaker. All tenses can be used in *Active* or *Passive forms*. If the *person* in the sentence is more important than the *object* the sentence is *active*. If the *object* is more important than the *person* then the sentence is *passive*.

 Examples:
Active:
He built this house in 2009.
Il a construit cette maison en 2009.

Passive:
This house was built in 2009.
Cette maison a été construite en 2009.

In English and French you use the verb "*to be/être*" followed by the *past participle* to state a *Passive tense*. Although in French when using a *Passive tense* it is necessary to correspond le *participe passé* to the sujet/objet in the sentence depending on if the object is masculin, féminin, or pluriel. See examples below.

 Note: If the sujet/objet is *singulier et masculin* in a *Passive tense* le *participe passé* stays the same.

 Examples:
Active:
My son drew a truck yesterday.
Mon fils a dessiné un camion hier.

Passive:
The truck was drawn yesterday.
Le camion a été dessiné hier.

 Note: If the sujet/objet is *singulier et féminin* in a *Passive tense* you need to add an "*e*" to le *participe passé.*

 Examples:
Active:
The maid is cleaning the room now.
Elle est en train de nettoyer la chambre.

Passive:
The room is being cleaned now.
La chambre est en train d'être nettoyée.

 Note: If the sujet/objet is *pluriel et masculin* in a *Passive tense* you need to add an "*s*" to le *participe passé.*

 Examples:
Active:
We will tear down the bridges Friday.
Nous démolirons les ponts vendredi.

Passive:
The bridges will be torn down Friday.
Les ponts seront démolis vendredi.

 Note: If the sujet/objet is *pluriel et féminin* in a *Passive tense* you need to add an "*es*" to le *participe passé.*

 Examples:
Active:
I have eaten all the apples.
J'ai mangé toutes les pommes.

Passive:
All the apples have been eaten.
Toutes les pommes ont été mangées.

Gerunds

What is a *gerund?* In English a *gerund* is the *present participle* used as a *subject* or *object* of a sentence. While in French un *gerondif* is le *verbe infinitif* used as a *sujet* ou *objet* of a sentence.

Examples used as a *subject* :

Playing soccer is fun.
Jouer au soccer est amusant.

Eating is necessary to live.
Manger est nécessaire pour vivre.

Doing the dishes is not fun.
Faire la vaisselle n'est pas amusant.

Speaking a second language is difficult.
Parler une deuxième langue est difficile.

Reading is necessary.
Lire est nécessaire.

Walking is good for your health.
Marcher est bon pour votre santé.

Feeding the dog is a challenge.
Nourrir le chien est un défi.

Working in Canada is cold.
Travailler au Canada est froid.

Examples used as an *object* :

Instead of walking, we drove.
Au lieu de marcher, nous avons conduit.

She is guilty of stealing the car.
Elle est coupable d'avoir volé la voiture.

I am used to working eight hours a day.
J'ai l'habitude de travailler huit heures.

I am looking forward to seeing my friend.
J'ai hâte de voir mon ami ce soir.

I am sorry for being late.
Je suis désolé d'être en retard.

He speaks about flying an airplane.
Il parle de piloter un avion.

I am worried about losing my keys.
Je suis inquiet de perdre mes clés.

Thank you for coming.
Merci de venir.

When you have the sentence structure "*subject + verb + adjective + preposition* " then the *preposition* is followed by a *gerund.* This is known as a *COI* in French or "*complément d'objet indirect* " which is found by asking the question "*à quoi/à qui, de quoi/de qui* " "*to what/whom* " or "*for what/whom* " after the adjective. For examples of *COI's* see unit 64.

Complément d'objet Direct and Indirect (COD) and (COI) better known today as CD and CI.

_____

In English and in French there are *complément d'objet direct* and *indirect*. This is found when asking a simple question after the first verb in the sentence.

Note: The *object* in the sentence is a *COD* when you ask "*quoi ou qui*" "*what or who*" after the first verb to find out it is the *object* in the sentence that receives the action.

Examples:

I bought a book yesterday.	I bought "what" yesterday?	a book	COD
J'ai acheté un livre hier.	J'ai acheté "quoi" hier?	un livre	COD
I had an exam last Monday.	I had "what" last Monday?	an exam	COD
J'ai eu un examen lundi passé.	J'ai eu "quoi" lundi passé?	un examen	COD
I picked up my son yesterday.	I picked up "who"?	my son	COD
Je suis allé chercher mon fils hier.	Je suis allé chercher "qui"?	mon fils	COD

Note: The *object* in the sentence is a *COI* when you ask "*à quoi/à qui ou de quoi/de qui*" after the first verb to find out it is "*to what/whom*" or "*for what/whom*" the action happens to.

Examples:

I can afford to buy it.	I can afford "to what"?	to buy it	COI
J'ai les moyens de l'acheter.	J'ai les moyens "de quoi?"	de l'acheter	COI
She finished studying.	She finished "to what?"	studying	COI
Elle a fini d'étudier.	Elle a fini "de quoi?"	d'étudier	COI
He continued speaking.	He continued "to what?"	speaking	COI
Il a continué de parler.	Il a continué "de quoi?"	de parler	COI

Note: When the sentence structure is "*subject + verb + adjective + preposition + COI*" in English and in French the COI is a *gerund/gerondif*.

Examples:

I am excited about going to Europe.   I am sorry for being late.
Je suis excité d'aller en Europe.   Je suis desolé d'être en retard.

I am worried about losing my job.   I will take care of sending it.
Je suis inquiet de perdre mon emploi.   Je prendrai soin de l'envoyer.

Phrasal Verbs

What is a *phrasal verb?* A *verb* is an action and a *phrase* is 2 or more words together that complete an idea of a sentence. Therefore a *phrasal verb* is a *verb* combined with 2 or more words to equal another verb. A verb combined with a *preposition* = *a phrasal verb.*

 Examples:

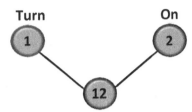

Turn On

Turn on = a verb or many verbs in French

Turn on = allumer/ouvrir/exciter

 Note: *Phrasal verbs* are something that cannot be translated word for word. You need to know the equivalent verb in French. If a *phrasal verb* is translated word for word it sounds like this:

 Examples:

Turn on the lights.
Tournez sur les lumières.

Open the lights.
Ouvrez les lumières.

 Note: *Phrasal verbs* in English have more than one meaning. There can be more than 2 and as many as 15 different reasons or 15 different verbs in French for one single *phrasal verb* in English.

It is also the same for verbs in French. There can be more than one meaning for a single verb.

 Examples:

Allumer = Allumer les lumières
Allumer = Allumer quelqu'un

Turn on = Turn on the lights
Turn on = Turn someone on

 Note: *Phrasal verbs* do *not* just stay in the *infinitive form* they can be conjugated into any tense; past, present or future.

 Note: You will need to have a good dictionary to find all the different situations that one *phrasal verb* is used.

 Note: When using a *phrasal verb* with an *object pronoun,* example "*me, you, him, her, it, us, you and them* " you need to separate the *phrasal verb* and put the *object pronoun* in between the *verb* and the *preposition.* See examples above.

Unit	
66	Verb Exceptions for using "*to be /être*" + ING (en train de)

___

In English and in French there are exceptions to verbs that are in *progress.*

 Note: You cannot say these verbs with "*to be + verb + ing.*" Vous ne pouvez pas dire ces verbes avec "*être + en train de + l'infintif.*"

Regular Verbs		Irregular Verbs	
Exceptions: believe	croire	forget	oublier
belong	appartenir	hear	entendre
hate	haïr	know	savoir/connaître
like	aimer	mean	vouloir dire
love	aimer	see	voir
need	avoir besoin	understand	comprendre
prefer	préférer		
realize	réaliser		
remember	se souvenir/se rappeler		
suppose	supposer		
want	vouloir		

 Note: Examples of what these verbs sound like if they are used in a *Continuous tense* are listed below.

 Examples:
I am wanting a coffee.
Je suis en train de vouloir un café.

I was knowing the answer when I was in class.
J'étais en train de connaître la réponse quand j'étais en classe.

To conjugate these verbs using the *Compound tenses* in French you need to use the verb *être* as the auxiliary and *not* the verb *avoir*.

Note: The verb *to have* is used in English for the conjugation of all the *Perfect tenses*. There are *no* exceptions like in French with these verbs. *Pronominal verbs* are also exceptions that will need to have the verb *être* as the auxiliary and *not* the verb *avoir*. For examples of *Pronominal verbs* see unit 49.

Exceptions:

D	devenir	devenu (e) (s)
R	rester	resté (e) (s)
M	monter	monté (e) (s)
R	retourner	retourné (e) (s)
S	sortir	sorti (e) (s)
V	venir	venu (e) (s)
A	aller	allé (e) (s)
N	naître	né (e) (s)
D	descendre	descendu (e) (s)
E	entrer	entré (e) (s)
R	revenir	revenu (e) (s)
T	tomber	tombé (e) (s)
R	rentrer	rentré (e) (s)
A	arriver	arrivé (e) (s)
M	mourir	mort (e) (s)
P	partir	parti (e) (s)

Examples:

Je suis allé (e)	I have gone
J'étais allé (e)	I had gone
Je serai allé (e)	I will have gone
Je serais allé (e)	I would have gone

Note: With these verbs in French you need to correspond le *participe passé* to le *sujet*. If le *sujet* is masculin le *participe passé* stays the same. If le *sujet* is feminin le *participe passé* will have an extra "*e*" added to it. If le *sujet* is masculin pluriel you need to add an "*s*" to le participe *passé*. If le sujet is féminin pluriel you need to add an "*es*" to le participe passé.

A *time clause* is a sentence that has two verbs that depend on each other. If the two actions are *connected* by *before, when, while, as soon as* or *until* there is a *connection* between the two actions therefore the sentence is considered a *time clause.*

 Examples:

I will give Joe the message when I see him.
Je donnerai le message à Joe quand je le verrai.

I will be making supper when you arrive.
Je serai en train de faire le souper lorsque tu arriveras.

I will have done my homework by the time you leave work.
J'aurai fait mes devoirs lorsque tu quitteras ton bureau.

 Note:

In French you need to use the *Future tense* of both verbs and *not* the *Present* and *Future tenses* as used in English if the 2nd action depends on the first; a *time clause.*

 Note:

In French it is possible to use the *présent du subjonctif* to equal a *time clause* in English. You are placing yourself in a *present moment* in the *future.*

 Examples:

Before I leave, I will call you.
Avant que je parte, je t'appellerai.

Before I read this book, I am going to watch the movie.
Avant que je lise ce livre, je vais voir le film.

 Note:

In English and in French if there is *no* connection between the verbs meaning they do *not* depend on each other the verbs will be seperated by "*and/et* " therefore both verbs are conjugated in the *Future tense* meaning the sentence is *not* a *time clause.*

 Examples:

I will make supper and he will do his homework.
Je ferai le souper et il fera ses devoirs.

A *tag question* is the *little question* that we all ask at the end of a statement. In French a *tag question* is "*n'est-ce pas?*" In English it is the same auxiliary used in the statement *only* in the opposite form. If the sentence is *negative* then the *tag question* is *positive,* if the sentence is *positive* then the *tag question* is *negative.*

 Examples:

You don't like peanuts, do you?
Vous n'aimez pas les arachides, n'est-ce pas?

They live in Québec, don't they?
Ils demeurent à Québec, n'est-ce pas?

You should study more, shouldn't you?
Tu devrais étudier plus, n'est-ce pas?

We didn't take the wrong exit, did we?
Nous n'avons pas pris la mauvaise sortie, n'est-ce pas?

It is Susan over there, isn't it?
C'est Susan là bas, n'est-ce pas?

Your mom makes your lunch, doesn't she?
Votre mère fait votre dîner, n'est-ce pas?

Your friends came over last night, didn't they?
Tes amis sont venus chez-toi hier soir, n'est-ce pas?

He couldn't be there, could he?
Il ne pouvait pas être là, n'est-ce pas?

 Note: When you use a *tag question* and your voice *goes down* you are *not* asking a question you are just trying to get the other person to see *eye to eye* with you. If your voice *goes up* it is a real question meaning you are *hoping* for an answer.

 Note: In English when using a *negative tag question* it is always in the contraction form. A list of contractions can be found in units 78 and 79.

Used to is used to talk about a _past routine_ whereas _to be used to_ is used to talk _about_ something that you are _accustomed to/habitué à_.

 In French you use _imparfait_ with "_habituellement_" to conjugate _used to_ as a _past routine._

 My mom used to clean the house on the weekends, but now she cleans the house on Mondays.
Ma mère nettoyait habituellement la maison les fins de semaine, mais maintenant elle nettoie la maison les lundis.

They used to go to church on Sundays, but not anymore.
Ils allaient habituellement à l'église les dimanches, mais ils n'y vont plus maintenant.

I used to play hockey Fridays, but now I play on Saturdays.
Je jouais habituellement au hockey les vendredis, mais maintenant je joue les samedis.

 This is different than telling someone what you are _used to_ today, what is _normal_ for you in the _present._

 I am used to working 40 hours a week.
J'ai l'habitude de travailler 40 heures par semaine.

We are used to going to Florida in the winter.
Nous avons l'habitude d'aller en Floride en hiver.

She is used to studying hard.
Elle a l'habitude de travailler dur.

A *Real Condition* means that the *condition* happens often in the *present.* You need to conjugate the first verb in the *Present tense* in English and in French following it with "*if/si* " then when the second verb happens it will be used in the *Present tense* as well. This makes the sentence become a *real condition.*

 Examples:

My dentist is happy if I visit him twice a year.
Mon dentiste est content si je le vois deux fois par année.

The dog usually barks if he hears someone at the door.
Le chien jappe habituellement s'il entend quelqu'un à la porte.

Isabelle gets upset if we talk in code.
Isabelle se fâche si nous parlons en code.

An *Unreal Condition* means that the *condition* has *not* yet happened or that it never happened. It can be used in the past or the future. In the past you did *not* know about the situation or did *not* have the means to do the action while in the future the *condition* needs to happen first before the action can be done.

 Examples:

I would have called if I had known there was an accident.
J'aurais appelé si j'avais su qu'il y avait un accident.

I would have done the dishes if I had had soap.
J'aurais fait la vaisselle si j'avais eu du savon.

I would buy a bigger house if I won the lottery.
J'achèterais une plus grande maison si je gagnais à la loterie.

I would go to Mexico if I had the time.
J'irais au Mexique si j'avais le temps.

 Note: If the *condition* is *unreal* and in the past then we start the sentence with the *Conditional Past* tense in English and in French, as the *condition* verb is conjugated using *Past Perfect* in English and using *plus-que-parfait* in French.

 Note: If the *condition* is *unreal* and is in the *present time* the first verb in English is the *Conditional Present* using the auxiliary *would* followed by the *base form* of a verb and the *condition verb* is used in the *Simple Past tense.* In French the tense *conditionnel présent* is used as the first verb whereas the *condition* verb is used with *imparfait.*

We often use *do* when we are talking about something that is very *general* meaning the action is *not* being *specified* as to what it is we *did, do* or *will do*. *Do* is for actions that can be considered *not* really exciting.

 Note: How many things can we *do* when we go to the gym?
How many things can we *do* when we clean the house?

 Examples: Examples for using "*do*"

I do my exercises five times a week.
Je fais mes exercices cinq fois par semaine.

I do the housework once a week.
Je fais le ménage une fois par semaine.

Do something.
Faire quelque chose.

What are you doing?
Qu'est ce-que tu fais là?

Do the best you can.
Faire de votre mieux.

He is doing his homework.
Il fait ses devoirs.

 Note: We use *make* when we can *produce* or *fabricate* something or when the action is *creative*.

 Examples: Examples for using "m*ake*"

I am making supper now.
Je fais le souper maintenant.

I will make a cake for your birthday.
Je ferai un gâteau pour votre anniversaire.

She makes several mistakes while speaking.
Elle fait plusieurs erreurs en parlant.

Make an appointment.
Prendre un rendez-vous.

Make money.
Faire de l'argent.

Make a phone call.
Faire un appel.

Some is *unknown* and is an *indefinite* number or quantity. *Any* is *known* and it does *not* matter which one quantity or part.

Note: Generally *some* is used in positive sentences whereas *any* is used in negative sentences. *Any* is used to determine the amount of something.

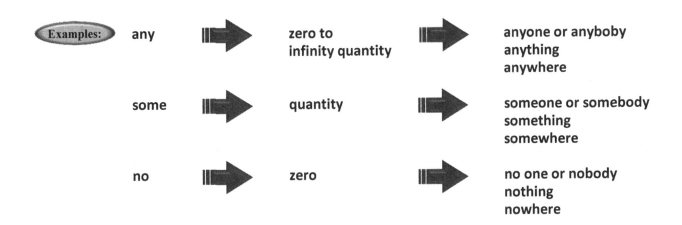

Examples: any ⟹ zero to infinity quantity ⟹ anyone or anyboby
anything
anywhere

some ⟹ quantity ⟹ someone or somebody
something
somewhere

no ⟹ zero ⟹ no one or nobody
nothing
nowhere

Examples:

I don't have any books.	Je n'ai pas de livres.
I have some books in my room.	J'ai des livres dans ma chambre.
I have nothing in my hands.	Je n'ai rien dans mes mains.

Is there anyone here?	Est-ce qu'il y a quelqu'un ici?
There is someone in my room.	Il y a quelqu'un dans ma chambre.
There is nobody here to help me.	Il n'y a personne ici pour m'aider.

Is there anything to do here?	Est-ce qu'il y a quelque chose à faire ici?
Yes, there is something to do.	Oui, il y a quelque chose que à faire.
There is nothing to do here.	Il n'y a rien à faire ici.

My book could be anywhere.	Mon livre pourrait être n'importe où.
My book is somewhere at home.	Mon livre est quelque part chez-moi.
There is nowhere to go and nowhere to hide.	Il n'y a nulle part où aller où se cacher.

When you use *tell* it is *directed* to the *person* you are speaking to. The *person* becomes important *not* the *words* in your statement.

When you use *say* it is *not directed* to the *person* you are speaking to. The *words* then become more important then the *person* you are talking to.

Examples:

I told Mary a secret.
J'ai dit un secret à Mary.

I will tell you the story later.
Je te dirai l'histoire plus tard.

I said "*see you tomorrow*" after class.
J'ai dit "*à demain*" après mon cours.

He always says that "*English is easy to learn.*"
Il dit toujours que "*l'anglais est facile à apprendre.*"

Note: When you use *talk* it is *informal* and is used to say something *directly* to someone whereas *speak* is *formal* and is used *indirectly* to speak to everyone or to a group.

Examples:

I will talk to my friend after class.
Je parlerai à mon ami après le cours.

I talked with my mom yesterday.
J'ai parlé à ma mère hier.

I spoke to Mr. St-Hilaire last week.
J'ai parlé à Mr. St-Hilaire la semaine passée.

I speak English and French.
Je parle anglais et français.

It is important to speak clearly to be understood.
C'est important de parler clairement pour être compris.

When you can replace the *subject* of the sentence with the adverb *who* which replaces the person's name, who becomes the *subject* of the sentence.

When you can replace the *subject* of the sentence with *who* you know the person that you are speaking about.

 Examples:

Who is at the door?	Qui est à la porte?
Jane is at the door.	Jane est à la porte.
Who made the mess?	Qui a fait le désordre?
Sam made the mess.	Sam a fait le désordre.
Who lives next door?	Qui demeure à côté?
Walter lives next door.	Walter demeure à côté.

 Note: *Who* is the *subject* of these sentences above.

When we use *whom* the *subject* is *not specified* it is very general and therefore the *subject* is present in the sentence and cannot be replaced.

 Examples:

To whom it may concern.
À qui de droit.

The man whom I spoke with was the CEO.
L'homme à qui j'ai parlé était le directeur général.

When we use *much, many* and *a lot* known as quantifiers we are expressing a large number of objects seen. Whether you use *much, many* or *a lot* it depends on if the object is countable or *not.* The object is considered *countable* when you can count all the objects in front of you meaning you can change the object to its plural form. When the objects are *countable* you have a choice of using *many* or *a lot.*

 Examples:

Countable Nouns	Uncountable Nouns
pens	water
glasses	time
tables	money
dogs	sand
cars	coffee

 Examples:

There are many books here.	Il y a beaucoup de livres ici.
There are a lot of books here.	Il y a beaucoup de livres ici.
There are not many books here.	Il n'y a pas beaucoup de livres ici.
There are not a lot of books here.	Il n'y a pas beaucoup de livres ici.
Are there many books here?	Est-ce qu'il y a beaucoup de livres ici?
Are there a lot of books here?	Est-ce qu'il y a beaucoup de livres ici?

 Note: When we cannot count something it is considered *uncountable.* If the object is *uncountable* then you have a choice of using *much* or *a lot* but *only* in *negative sentences* or *questions* never in *affirmative sentences.* You can *only* use *a lot* in *positive sentences* with *uncountable* nouns.

 Examples:

There is a lot of milk left.	Il reste beaucoup de lait.
There is not much milk.	Il n'y a pas beaucoup de lait.
There is not a lot of milk.	Il n'y a pas beaucoup de lait.
Is there much milk left?	Est-ce qu'il y a beaucoup de lait qui reste?
Is there a lot of milk left?	Est-ce qu'il y a beaucoup de lait qui reste?

 Note:

The mistake is if you say:	The correct sentence is:
Exceptions: There is much milk.	There is a lot of milk.

Verbs that end with:

f	h	k	p	s	x	ch	sh

When you add "*ed*" to these verbs it sounds like a "*t*"

Examples:

ask	asked (t)
stop	stopped (t)
watch	watched (t)

Verbs that end with:

b	e	g	l	m	n	r	v	y	z

When you add "*ed*" to these verbs it sounds like a "*d*"

Examples:

answer	answered (d)
arrive	arrived (d)
call	called (d)

Verbs that end with:

d	t

When you add "*ed*" to these verbs it sounds like "*id*"

Examples:

end	ended (id)
want	wanted (id)
heat	heated (id)

Contractions are a shorter version of the words written or spoken where letters have been *eliminated* or *left out*. *Negative contractions* using *not* are frequently used in English however in French they are used with *ne* changing to *n'* when used with a verb that starts with a *vowel*. *Contractions* in English are used with the *subject* and the *auxiliary* combined or the *auxiliary* and the *negation* combined by an *apostrophe*. See unit 79 for *negative contractions* in English.

Examples:

I am	=	I'm	I have	=	I've	I had	=	I'd
You are	=	You're	You have	=	You've	You had	=	You'd
He is	=	He's	He has	=	He's	He had	=	He'd
We are	=	We're	We have	=	We've	We had	=	We'd
You are	=	You're	You have	=	You've	You had	=	You'd
They are	=	They're	They have	=	They've	They had	=	They'd

I will	=	I'll	I would	=	I'd	Where is	=	Where's
You will	=	You'll	You would	=	You'd	Who is	=	Who's
He will	=	He'll	He would	=	He'd	What is	=	What's
We will	=	We'll	We would	=	We'd	There is	=	There's
You will	=	You'll	You would	=	You'd	That is	=	That's
They will	=	They'll	They would	=	They'd			

Note: When using the *contraction* " *'d* " or " *'s* " be careful as they have a *double meaning*. The " *'d* "could mean the auxiliary *had* or the auxiliary *would*. The " *'s* "could mean the auxiliary *is* or the auxiliary *has*.

Examples:

I had taken	=	I'd taken	past participle used after *had*	=	J'avais pris
I would take	=	I'd take	the base form used after *would*	=	Je prendrais
He is taking	=	He's taking	*is* + base form of a verb + ing	=	Il prend
He has taken	=	He's taken	past participle used after *has*	=	Il a pris

In French *contractions* are used more with *articles* and *prepositions* or when two words beside each other each have a vowel where *le* ou *la* + a word staring with a vowel or a silent letter like *h* becomes " *l'* ". With *negative* sentences the *ne becomes n'* when a verb starts with a vowel. See examples below.

Examples:

Words	Articiles/Prepositions	Verbs
l'auto	à + le = au	Je + aime = J'aime
l'usine	à + les = aux	Je + accepte = J'accepte
l'hotel	de + le = du	Je + ne + aime pas = Je n'aime pas
l'avion	de + les + des	Ce + est = C'est

Again, *contractions* are a shorter version of the words written or spoken where letters have been *eliminated* or *left out.*

I am not	=	I'm not	I have not	=	I haven't
You are not	=	You're not	You have not	=	You haven't
He is not	=	He isn't	He has not	=	He hasn't
We are not	=	We aren't	We have not	=	We haven't
You are not	=	You're not	You have not	=	You haven't
They are not	=	They aren't	They have not	=	They haven't
I was not	=	I wasn't	I had not	=	I hadn't
You were not	=	You weren't	You had not	=	You hadn't
He was not	=	He wasn't	He had not	=	He hadn't
We were not	=	We weren't	We had not	=	We hadn't
You were not	=	You weren't	You had not	=	You hadn't
They were not	=	They weren't	They had not	=	They hadn't
I do not	=	I don't	I did not	=	I didn't
You do not	=	You don't	You did not	=	You didn't
He does not	=	He doesn't	He did not	=	He didn't
We do not	=	We don't	We did not	=	We didn't
You do not	=	You don't	You did not	=	You didn't
They do not	=	They don't	They did not	=	They didn't
I will not	=	I won't	I cannot	=	I can't
You will not	=	You won't	You cannot	=	You can't
He will not	=	He won't	He cannot	=	He can't
We will not	=	We won't	We cannot	=	We can't
You will not	=	You won't	You cannot	=	You can't
They will not	=	They won't	They cannot	=	We can't
I would not	=	I wouldn't	I could not	=	I couldn't
You would not	=	You wouldn't	You could not	=	You couldn't
He would not	=	He wouldn't	He could not	=	He couldn't
We would not	=	We wouldn't	We could not	=	We couldn't
You would not	=	You wouldn't	You could not	=	You couldn't
They would not	=	They wouldn't	They could not	=	They couldn't
I should not	=	I shouldn't	That is not	=	That's not
You should not	=	You shouldn't	That is not	=	That isn't
He should not	=	He shouldn't	There is not	=	There's not
We should not	=	We shouldn't	There is not	=	There isn't
You should not	=	You shouldn't	There are not	=	There aren't
They should not	=	They shouldn't	That was not	=	That wasn't

Note: In French these *contractions* don't exist. You have to use "*ne* " "*pas* " see unit 78.

Object pronouns me/moi/me, you/toi/te, him/lui/le, her/elle/la/lui, it/le/la, us/nous, you/vous, them/eux/elles/leur/les are used so the _noun_ does _not_ have to be repeated in the sentence. In English and in French it is possible to replace the _object_ in the sentence with a _direct object pronoun_ or an _indirect object pronoun._

Direct objects answer the question _to whom/to what, à quoi/à qui_ the subject is carrying out. A _direct object pronoun_ replaces the _noun_ in the sentence. In English the _direct object pronoun_ is normally placed _after_ the first verb whereas in French it is before the verb.

 Examples:

I wash my truck every week.
Je lave mon camion chaque semaine.

I wash it every week.
Je le lave chaque semaine.

I file the documents often.
Je classe les documents souvent.

I file them often.
Je les classe souvent.

Indirect objects state _for who/for whom, de quoi/de qui_ the subject is doing something. In English an _indirect object pronoun_ replaces an _indirect noun_ and is normally placed _after_ the verb. In French however it is placed after the _subjet._

 Examples:

I gave a gift to my mom yesterday.
J'ai donné un cadeau à ma mère hier.

I gave her a gift yesterday.
Je lui a donné un cadeau hier.

He sends Jane a letter every day.
Il envoie à Jane une lettre chaque jour.

He sends her a letter every day.
Il lui envoie une lettre chaque jour.

The _adverbial pronoun_ "y" means "_there_" when the _location_ has already been mentioned in the sentence. "_Y_" also means "_it_" or "_them._"

 Examples:

I will be at work later.
Je serai au travail plus tard.

I will be there later.
J'y serai plus tard.

I am going to my doctor's office.
Je vais au bureau de mon médecin.

I am going there after work.
J'y vais après mon travail.

The _pronoun "en"_ replaces the _things/objects_ already mentioned in the sentence. The _pronoun en_ in French replaces "_de ou du + un objet_" in the sentence. In English it is used as "_some + an object_ or _any + an object._"

I would like some coffee.
J'aimerais avoir du café.

I would like some.
J'aimerais en avoir.

You don't have any butter.
Tu n'as pas de beurre.

You don't have any.
Tu n'en as pas.

Irregular Verbs

Base Form	Past Tense	Past Participle	French Verb
arise	arose	arisen	survenir
awake	awakened/awoke	awakened/awoken	se réveiller
be	was, were	been	être
bear	bore	born/borne	supporter
beat	beat	beaten/beat	battre
become	became	become	devenir
begin	began	begun	commencer
bend	bent	bent	courber
bet	bet	bet	parier
bid	bid	bid	faire une offre
bind	bound	bound	lier
bite	bit	bitten	mordre
bleed	bled	bled	saigner
blow	blew	blown	souffler
break	broke	broken	briser/casser
breed	bred	bred	élever
bring	brought	brought	apporter
build	built	built	construire
burn	burned/burnt	burned/burnt	brûler
burst	burst	burst	éclater
buy	bought	bought	acheter
cast	cast	cast	jeter
catch	caught	caught	attraper
choose	chose	chosen	choisir
cling	clung	clung	se cramponner
come	came	come	venir
cost	cost	cost	coûter
creep	crept	crept	ramper
cut	cut	cut	couper
deal	dealt	dealt	traiter
dig	dug	dug	creuser
dive	dove/dived	dived	plonger
do	did	done	faire
draw	drew	drawn	dessiner
dream	dreamed/dreamt	dreamed/dreamt	rêver
drink	drank	drunk	boire
drive	drove	driven	conduire
eat	ate	eaten	manger

Irregular Verbs

Base Form	Past Tense	Past Participle	French Verb
fall	fell	fallen	tomber
feed	fed	fed	nourrir
feel	felt	felt	ressentir
fight	fought	fought	combattre
find	found	found	trouver
fit	fit	fit	ajuster
flee	fled	fled	fuir
fling	flung	flung	lancer
fly	flew	flown	voler (avion)
forecast	forecast	forecast	prévoir
forget	forgot	forgotten/forgot	oublier
forgive	forgave	forgiven	pardonner
freeze	froze	frozen	geler
get	got	gotten/ got	obtenir
give	gave	given	donner
go	went	gone	aller
grind	ground	ground	moudre/grincer
grow	grew	grown	pousser
hang	hung	hung	pendre/accrocher
have	had	had	avoir
hear	heard	heard	entendre
hide	hid	hidden	cacher
hit	hit	hit	frapper
hold	held	held	tenir
hurt	hurt	hurt	blesser
keep	kept	kept	garder
kneel	knelt/kneeled	knelt/kneeled	s'agenouiller
knit	knitted/knit	knitted/knit	tricoter
know	knew	known	savoir
lay	laid	laid	poser/mettre
lead	led	led	mener
lean	leaned/leant	leaned/leant	pencher
leap	leaped / leapt	leaped/leapt	bondir
learn	learned/learnt	learned/learnt	apprendre
leave	left	left	partir/quitter
lend	lent	lent	prêter
let	let	let	laisser
lie	lay	lain	s'allonger

Irregular Verbs

Base Form	Past Tense	Past Participle	French Verb
light	lit/lighted	lit/lighted	allumer
lose	lost	lost	perdre
make	made	made	faire
mean	meant	meant	signifier
meet	met	met	rencontrer
mistake	mistook	mistaken	se méprendre sur
misunderstand	misunderstood	misunderstood	comprendre mal
mow	mowed	mowed/mown	tondre/faucher
pay	paid	paid	payer
prove	proved	proven/proved	prouver
put	put	put	mettre/poser
quit	quit/quitted	quit/quitted	démissionner
read	read	read	lire
redo	redid	redone	refaire
rid	rid	rid	se débarrasser
ride	rode	ridden	monter (cheval/vélo)
ring	rang	rung	sonner
rise	rose	risen	se lever
run	ran	run	courir
say	said	said	dire
see	saw	seen	voir
seek	sought	sought	chercher
sell	sold	sold	vendre
send	sent	sent	envoyer
set	set	set	placer
sew	sewed	sewn/sewed	coudre
shake	shook	shaken	secouer
shave	shaved	shaved/shaven	se raser
shear	sheared	sheared/shorn	tondre
shed	shed	shed	verser (larme)
shine	shined/shone	shined/shone	briller
shoot	shot	shot	tirer
show	showed	shown/showed	montrer
shrink	shrank/shrunk	shrunk	rétrécir
shut	shut	shut	fermer
sing	sang	sung	chanter
sink	sank/sunk	sunk	sombrer
sit	sat	sat	s'asseoir

Irregular Verbs

Base Form	Past Tense	Past Participle	French Verb
sleep	slept	slept	dormir
slide	slid	slid	glisser
sling	slung	slung	hisser/lancer
slit	slit	slit	inciser
smell	smelled/smelt	smelled/smelt	sentir
sow	sowed	sown/sowed	semer
speak	spoke	spoken	parler
speed	sped/speeded	sped/speeded	rouler trop vite
spell	spelled/spelt	spelled/spelt	épeler
spend	spent	spent	dépenser/passer(temps)
spill	spilled/spilt	spilled/spilt	renverser
spin	spun	spun	tournoyer
split	split	split	diviser
spoil	spoiled/spoilt	spoiled/spoilt	gâter
spread	spread	spread	étendre/étaler
spring	sprang/sprung	sprung	bondir
stand	stood	stood	être debout
steal	stole	stolen	voler/piquer
stick	stuck	stuck	coller
sting	stung	stung	piquer
strike	struck	struck/stricken	frapper
string	strung	strung	suspendre
strive	strove/strived	striven/strived	s'efforcer
swear	swore	sworn	jurer
sweep	swept	swept	balayer
swell	swelled	swollen/swelled	enfler/grossir
swim	swam	swum	nager
swing	swung	swung	se balancer
take	took	taken	prendre
teach	taught	taught	enseigner
tear	tore	torn	déchirer
tell	told	told	dire
think	thought	thought	penser
throw	threw	thrown	lancer/jeter
understand	understood	understood	comprendre
wake	woke/waked	woken/waked	réveiller
wear	wore	worn	porter
weave	wove/weaved	woven/weaved	tisser

Irregular Verbs

Base Form	Past Tense	Past Participle	French Verb
win	won	won	gagner
wind	wound	wound	enrouler
withdraw	withdrew	withdrawn	retirer
withhold	withheld	withheld	retenir
withstand	withstood	withstood	résister
wring	wrung	wrung	tordre
write	wrote	written	écrire

Glossary

Adjective
is a word that describes a noun
Adverb
a word that describes a verb
Articles
in grammar a word such as "a, an, the"
Auxiliary
is used to indicate a tense, voice or mood
Base form of a verb
The base form of the verb is the infinitive without the "to"
«*Bescherelle* »
A book of conjugated verbs in French
Comparisons
to observe the similarities or differences in an object
or verb
Complement d'objet Direct
the object which receives the action of the verb
Complement d'objet Indirect
to relfect to whom or to what the action occurs
Conjugation
the changing of a verb to reflect the tense
Conditional
expressing a condition which something else depends on
example; "if"
Contractions
a short form of words
Countable
something that is able to be counted
Duration
the length of time that something lasts
Formula
a plan or a set of rules for conjugating verb tenses
Gerund
in grammar the present participle form of the verb
used as a subject or an object
Infinitive
is the raw form of the verb without conjugation and
without a subject

Glossary

Modal Auxiliaries
used to express a mood
Negative
expressing a refusal or denial lacking positive qualities
Object
something that can be touched or seen
Phrasal Verbs
a verb combined with a preposition
Phrase
a group of words that complete an idea of a sentence
Possessive Adjectives
to modify a noun to make it belong to someone or something
Preposition
a word used to relate words to other words
Pronoun
a word that replaces a noun
Questions
words addressed to a person to obtain an answer
Subject
a word that represents a person or thing doing the action
Subjunctive
may be used for grammatically subordinate statements or questions
Superlatives
the highest quality of adjectives or adverbs
Syllables
a part of a word that is pronounced as a single unit
Tag questions
a little question at the end of a statement
Time clauses
Time clauses are used to indicate the time
that an event in the main clause takes place
Uncountable
something that is not countable
Verbs
a word that is used to indicate action